Building
COMMUNITY

THOMAS W. KOPF

A Service of

NAHB

BuilderBooks.com™
National Association of Home Builders
1201 15th Street, NW
Washington, DC 20005-2800
(800) 223-2665
www.builderbooks.com

LIVEGATHERPLAY

Building Community
Thomas W. Kopf

Theresa Minch	Executive Editor
Jenny Stewart	Assistant Editor
Sharon Hamm	Copyeditor
E Design Communications	Cover Designer

BuilderBooks at the National Association of Home Builders

THERESA MINCH	Executive Editor
DORIS M. TENNYSON	Senior Acquisitions Editor
JESSICA POPPE	Assistant Editor
JENNY STEWART	Assistant Editor
BRENDA ANDERSON	Director of Fulfillment
GILL WALKER	Marketing Manager
JACQUELINE BARNES	Marketing Manager
GERALD HOWARD	NAHB Executive Vice President and CEO
MARK PURSELL	Executive Vice President Marketing & Sales
GREG FRENCH	Staff Vice President, Publications and Affinity Programs

ISBN 0-86718-594-5

© 2004 by BuilderBooks™
of the National Association of Home Builders
of the United States of America

Printed in the United States of America

Library of Congress Cataloging-in-Publication Data

Kopf, Tom, 1955-
  Building community / Tom Kopf.
    p. cm.
  ISBN 0-86718-594-5
  1. Community development. 2. Homesites. 3. City planning. I. Title.

HN49.C6K66 2003
307.1'4—dc22

2003020483

Disclaimer
This publication is designed to provide accurate and authoritative information in regard to the subject matter covered. It is sold with the understanding that the publisher is not engaged in rendering legal, accounting, or other professional service. If legal advice or other expert assistance is required, the services of a competent professional person should be sought.
   —From a Declaration of Principles jointly adopted by a Committee of the American Bar Association and a Committee of Publishers and Associations.

For further information, please contact:
BuilderBooks™
National Association of Home Builders
1201 15th Street, NW
Washington, DC 20005-2800
(800) 223-2665
Check us out online at: www.builderbooks.com

12/03 E Design/Circle/Good 2000

About the Author

Thomas W. Kopf is a Partner in DTJ DESIGN, Inc., a 90-person multidiscipline firm located in Boulder, Colorado. DTJ offers community planning, residential and commercial architecture, and landscape architecture services to clients nationwide. As a planner and landscape architect, Thomas has specialized in residential community design since 1978. His thoughtful design approach considers both the needs of the developer, and the desires of the marketplace. At DTJ DESIGN, Thomas leads many of the design teams seeking innovative and cost-effective solutions for places to live, gather and play.

Thomas has written numerous articles on community design, and his work has been featured in *Professional Builder*, *Builder*, and *Land Development* magazines. He is a frequent seminar speaker for the National Association of Home Builders and has participated in the Land Planning workshops for more than 16 years. Thomas was instrumental in creating DTJ DESIGN's position paper on Smart Growth, which has been distributed by ULI; and has been the keynote speaker for the Baton Rouge Growth Coalition's Smart Growth Awards program. In addition, he has judged the Best in American Living Awards and the South Florida's BEST Awards.

Acknowledgments

Writing *Building Community* has been a major endeavor, and extremely enjoyable. Credit must be given to those that made a significant contribution and made my job easier. First, and foremost, are the many talented designers at DTJ DESIGN who produce such terrific and meaningful work. I am continuously impressed with the attention to detail and quality that everyone achieves. Second, an immense debt of gratitude is due my Partner, Steve James, and Associate, Chris Moore, for their thought-provoking and insightful comments on the first draft. Their dedication to the effort made the work better, and more useful to the reader. Third, it is necessary to thank the many clients whose projects appear in the book. Their commitment to building community is evident in the work they allowed us to do. I hope that the reader will take the time to visit some of the communities discussed in the book to enjoy what these builders and developers have created.

I also appreciate the comments of Partners Rick Volpe and Dave Williams and Associate Susan Wade who provided input on specific chapters of the book; our intern, Stephanie Voss who provided me a student's perspective; and Associates Scott Pessin and Shelly Gabel who spent many hours making sure the graphics communicated the intent. Debbie Bassert, NAHB's Director of Land Development Services acted as a sounding board throughout the project, and for that, I am grateful.

Special thanks go to my Executive Editor, Theresa Minch, and Assistant Editor, Jenny Stewart, both of BuilderBooks, whose guidance and input throughout the process was invaluable. This book would not have been possible without the support of NAHB's Land Developers Committee under the guidance of Chairman Bruce Boncke. NAHB staff Ed Tombari's assistance in reviewing the manuscript and providing input is also appreciated. Thanks to all of you. And finally, thanks to my family for letting me take precious vacation time to work on the book.

BuilderBooks would like to thank Bob Kaufman, Bill Kreager, John Carmen, and Dave Ager for reviewing the manuscript.

Table of Contents

List of Figures

Chapter 1: The Art and Science of Building Community

Chapter 2: The Market

Chapter 3: Understanding Site Context

Chapter 4: Community Visioning

Chapter 5: Community Design

Chapter 6: Regulatory Issues and the Approval Process

Chapter 7: Paying for Community

Chapter 8: Marketing Community

Introduction

In nearly every city in America there is at least one neighborhood that exemplifies the concept of home and community. Often these are quiet tree lined streets, in a distinctive pattern, with architecture grounded in the spirit of the place. Buildings fit the site and the context. Civic buildings and open spaces provide texture and foster activity in the neighborhood. People come together with a shared interest in where they live, to make "community" more than a collection of buildings.

The heart of the community comes from the people within. It is the connections made by families of all types because they share a property line, or their children play together. It is more than the swimming pool, it's the swim team; and it's more than the neighborhood park it's the Fourth of July parade and it's more than the village green it's the farmer's market that allow these connections to be made. Creating places for something gives physical form to the idea of community. Events happen in the buildings and spaces we design and build. It is important that thoughtful design enrich these places. Community comes alive through these places and events. Community is where we live, gather and play.

The purpose of this book is to help the reader understand the importance of building community, what elements are necessary for community success and how to design a community that is sensitive to the environment, respects the neighbors, is a financial success and creates a delightful place. This book will help builders and developers understand what to look for in their design consultants, how to evaluate design product, how to make positive, constructive input during the design process, how to obtain approvals for their communities, and how the design of their communities impacts the value of the homes and communities they build. This will make their work more efficient and cost effective.

Figure I.1–3 Community comes alive through places and events.

Community designers can use this book to spark ideas and seek a fresh look at how their work impacts the built environment. It may challenge a conventional design approach, raising the bar and resulting in better communities. Better community design can change the public perceptions of growth and make it easier to obtain approvals and implement good design.

Design students in architecture, landscape architecture and planning will find this book useful as an instructional text establishing an advanced knowledge of site planning and community design principles. This book explores the relationships between the site, building design, the market, and community design and will make new graduates more valuable to professional practice design firms. This book will supplement other, more detailed, texts on ecology, horticulture, sociology, construction and engineering.

Community leaders can use this book to help builders and citizens understand what is expected from new development within their communities. This book will help cities realize a positive vision for their community design.

Chapter One: The Art and Science of Building Community, examines how the marriage of art and science is necessary to create outstanding communities. It presents a historical evolution from the simple need for shelter to a more mature need for human inter-relationships in an expanding economy. And finally, it presents the qualities and characteristics of community.

Chapter Two: The Market, covers the strategy and benefits of a residential market analysis and links various market segments to desired housing types, amenities and buyer preferences. This is followed by a detailed discussion of housing types, appropriate densities and site conditions, and common issues and solutions related to specific housing types.

Chapter Three: Understanding the Site, outlines the environmental and man-made influences on community building. It explores the natural environmental influences of soils, slopes, geology, climate, hydrology, vegetation, noise, and wildlife and the man-made influences of roads, access, water and sewer systems, dry utilities, land use, development regulation, historical and archeological assets, and community perceptions on the design of the community. The chapter presents approaches that balance these competing influences and how these elements can be woven into the community fabric. The importance of a site opportunities and constraints summary is discussed and two important concepts are introduced.

Chapter Four: Visioning describes in detail how to bring a community idea to life in the minds of the builder, the regulators, and the buyers. It explains the importance of a community story in both the design and marketing of the community. It illustrates how plans, sketches, elevations, text, and models can be combined to paint a picture of the future community. And finally, it discusses how to implement the community vision through design guidelines, Home Owners Associations, and builder commitment.

Chapter Five: Community Design is the heart of the book. It suggests that successful community design is the result of a passion for community, a process that generates great ideas and a development pattern that responds to site context. It describes a process that begins with design goals that guide the creation of the community through the site analysis, market analysis and visioning as it evolves into first concept ideas, and than more detailed concept plans. The chapter discusses several design elements that define help express community, including texture of land uses and architecture, massing, contrast, and color. The chapter concludes with a description of six main community design strategies and a case study illustrating each approach. The six community design strategies include open space

Credit: DTJ Design.

Figure I.4 Live.   **Figure I.5 Gather.**   **Figure I.6 Play.**

communities, amenity based communities, traditional neighborhood development, blended communities, mixed use communities and urban infill.

Chapter Six: Regulatory Issues and the Approval Process begins with a discussion of the barriers to quality community design from the perspective of the builder and the regulators. While controversial, it is necessary to explore these barriers and make an honest evaluation of the impact of our role in the growth debate. Understanding each stakeholders unique issues encourages groups to seek common ground and work toward appropriate development solutions. The chapter presents eight tips for more effective processing to help builders and developers obtain the necessary community design approvals.

Chapter Seven: Paying for Community explores the value that can be received from creating a sense of community and will help the builder and developer establish the appro-priate budgets to guide development. Special districts, metropolitan districts and tax increment districts are discussed as possible vehicles to finance community.

The final chapter, Chapter Eight: Marketing Community, describe how the builder and developer best take advantage of the sense of community they have built. It presents a strategy to effectively use the press, the benefits of community events on creating interest and excitement about the community, the types of collateral materials that should be created, and how community life can become a powerful sales tool.

Each of these chapters is designed to walk the reader through the community building process and describe the benefits that can be gained from implementing community building. It is important to remember that in developing communities we are creating places that will last generations. We have a responsibility to complete that work in the best way possible.

CHAPTER 1
The Art and Science of Building Community

The Art of Community Design

Much like the composition of a beautiful painting, a well-designed community is composed of colors and textures and massing in such a way as to be pleasing to the eye, yet functional. Community designers use the features of the existing site, building shapes, colors, materials and styles, road widths and materials, natural and man-made amenities, and landscape as the palette from which they create their composition. To create the best communities, designers must give special care to the contrast of uses and definition of edges, focus on key elements of the composition, and provide attention to detail.

In addition to the aesthetic qualities of the community, thought must be given to the social qualities that define where people live. The combination is what makes the composition come to life. Together, the physical design and the community life bring people together in a way that makes a house a home and a neighborhood a place of friends. Excellent community design encourages people to move beyond the comfort and safety of their house and enjoy other people and the environment around them.

Together, the physical design and the community life bring people together in a way that makes a house a home and a neighborhood a place of friends.

The ability to create a well-composed community is a practiced art that requires the energy and foresight of more than just the designer. Like the patron of Michelangelo's time, the builder and developer must have an appreciation for the value of good design. And as with the Sistine Chapel (Figure 1.1) this value can be immediate and last for a long time. The team brings the patron's dream and vision to light and helps make it a reality. When they've done this job well, the builder and developer can enjoy the benefits through rapid appreciation and an enhanced reputation.

The Science of Community Design

To stand the test of time, a community must be built on a good foundation. This foundation rests on an understanding of the physical nature and properties of the natural environment, and on the materials that compose the built environment. This science has evolved over time through more precise scientific instruments, more in-depth study, and the development of new construction materials and methods. The community builder and the community design team must be up-to-date regarding the science of each element that has an impact on the natural and built environment.

The natural environment comprises a myriad of interrelated elements that influence design. Soils must be strong enough to hold up roads or buildings, or those constructions may expand when wet. Ground water can exert tremendous pressure on foundation walls, and freeze/thaw cycles can destroy roads within a few days. Vegetation can slow water, thereby reducing erosion, or natural drainage channels can flood, resulting in loss of property and life. Climate, wildlife, topography, and geology are a few of the other elements that influence the built community. The study of ecology explores the interrelationship of these various elements.

When properly understood, natural elements can be incorporated into the plan, creating value for adjacent property, or mitigated to eliminate long-term problems. When misunderstood, these elements can add significant costs and delays to development, which will raise the price of homes. Problems can continue over time, which will inconvenience homeowners and increase the cost of maintenance.

Science and engineering improve our built environment through new materials and construction methods. With the exception of key changes, many of the systems we take for granted, such as roads, water, and sanitary sewer, have remained essentially the same for decades. *Lime treating* and *curb under-drains* minimize moisture

Figure 1.1 The Creation of Adam, by Michelangelo.

Credit: Courtesy of SuperStock, Inc.

damage to roadways. Storm drainage techniques, such as *bioswales* (Figure 1.2) and *water-quality ponds*, have significantly improved water quality. Water and sewer lines are made of *PVC* instead of concrete, thus making construction easier. Pipeline maintenance is now performed by remote-controlled robots, which run the length of the line extruding a synthetic lining and come back to cut holes for laterals. Work that once took weeks of digging and reinstalling pipe can now be completed in a matter of hours. In short, science is making our communities more functional, durable, and cost effective.

The Interface between Art and Science

To assume that, because science and engineering have such an important role in community development, all design decisions should default to the most cost-effective and efficient method is a mistake. Most important is that a balance be struck between the value created through sensitivity to the natural environment, respect for the neighbors, and amenities that meet the needs of the buyers, and the most cost-effective way to build. Building community is the weaving together of multiple influences through an integrated process of architecture, landscape architecture, and planning. The community designer must prioritize each element or influence that affects design, and weigh the costs and benefits of each against the community as a whole.

Straight, grid streets may yield the most lots, but they rarely provide the visual diversity found in more charming neighborhoods. *Single-loaded* streets may raise the development cost per lot, yet this increased cost may

be more than offset by the lot premiums for homes facing an open space. The visual impact of higher-density homes may be mitigated by additional amenities or landscaping. So, too, a lack of amenities might result in slow absorption and a poor reputation for the builder. Too many homes of the same size, shape, and color may delay project approvals and result in poor acceptance in the marketplace. Architectural diversity might cost slightly more, but the individuality creates a pride of ownership that translates into higher values and makes a community more visually interesting. Each decision affects the success of the project and must be carefully considered within the context of the site, the buyer, and the financial implications. Without the proper balance of art and science, the community will not achieve its full potential.

Historical Context

From the dawn of man, people have been drawn to each other for companionship, protection, and sharing the tasks of survival. Shelter has always been a basic need. For many since the industrial revolution in the mid-1800s, shelter meant living in cramped quarters with none of the conveniences we find essential today. Tenements were overcrowded and filthy, with limited or no sanitary facilities. Buildings were close together, minimizing ventilation, and rotting garbage lined the gutters. People worked in equally dreadful conditions, breathing pollutants from the coal-fired industrial equipment.

Only the privileged few had the resources to purchase land and build large homes. The wealthy had transportation options. Business owners could have the benefit of a country

Figure 1.2 A bioswale filters runoff from an adjacent parking area.

estate, while factory workers were forced to live in the city. In the 1840s, the life expectancy at birth for those living in the country was 15 years longer than for those living in the city.

Early Community Design

As early as 1813, Robert Owens, a Manchester textile industrialist, conceived of building communities for his workers. He theorized that better living conditions would result in happier and more productive employees. His ideas of better housing and open spaces were well received by his workers at the mill in New Lanark, in southern Scotland. Although many of his peers scoffed at the idea of using company profits to improve the lives of workers, others—notably, Sir Titus Salt, who established Saltaire (1853) along the River Aire in Yorkshire, England—heeded the lessons of Robert Owens. That there were economic benefits to be had from making this investment in the lives of their workers became apparent. Soon thereafter, the Cadbury Brothers and the Lever Brothers Company also built company towns at Bournville (1879) (Figure 1.3) and Port Sunlight (1887), respectively.

Figure 1.3 Typical architectural detailing in the company town of Bournville.

These new towns were designed from the beginning to provide employment, services, community gardens, and open spaces. Initially, the towns were limited in size, intended specifically to provide housing for the factory's workers. But in 1894, George Cadbury began building on newly acquired land adjacent to Bournville and offered housing for people not employed at the chocolate factory. Residents enjoyed individual yards as well as public open spaces, and Bournville was a desirable place to live. This fact was not lost on Ebenezer Howard, whose Garden City ideas formed the basis for open space community design. Howard had been considering how to improve the living conditions in cities and towns.

In 1902, Howard republished his original thesis as a small book titled *Garden Cities of Tomorrow*. He envisioned an urban system that co-existed with rural life, thus providing the opportunities of a town with the open space and food supply of the country (Figure 1.4). Many of Howard's guiding principles are still valid today. These principles include the following:

- proper scale
- regional growth by a process of colonization
- a balanced community of work and residence
- open area owned by the community as a whole
- a simple organic pattern to separate conflicting land use
- relatively low density and spatial containment by the use of an agricultural open space

In 1919, the Garden City and Town Planning Association defined Garden Cities as:

a town designed for healthy living and industry; of a size that makes possible a full measure of social life, but not larger; surrounded by a rural belt; the whole of the land being in public ownership or being held in trust for the community.

This organization grew from an interest in the work of Ebenezer Howard and was devoted to promoting garden cities in England and Scotland.

Howard's vision for a Garden City was that it would encompass about 6,000 acres, with approximately 1,000 acres devoted to a central village. The village would be anchored by a public park encircled by civic buildings. A Grand Avenue would connect neighborhoods within the community, linking residential areas to the village core. The village would be home to about 30,000 people living in approximately 5,500 buildings. An additional 2,000 people would live in the agricultural district surrounding the village. Neighborhoods would be anchored by schools, churches, and parks, none more than 240 yards from any house. Warehouses and factories would be located on the outer ring of the village and serviced by a rail line. When this theoretical size was achieved, a new Garden City would be started.

With the development of Letchworth (1903) and Welwyn Garden City (1919), it became apparent that the original vision for a Garden City could not accommodate the large numbers of people who wanted to live in this type of community. There simply were not enough industries available to become the

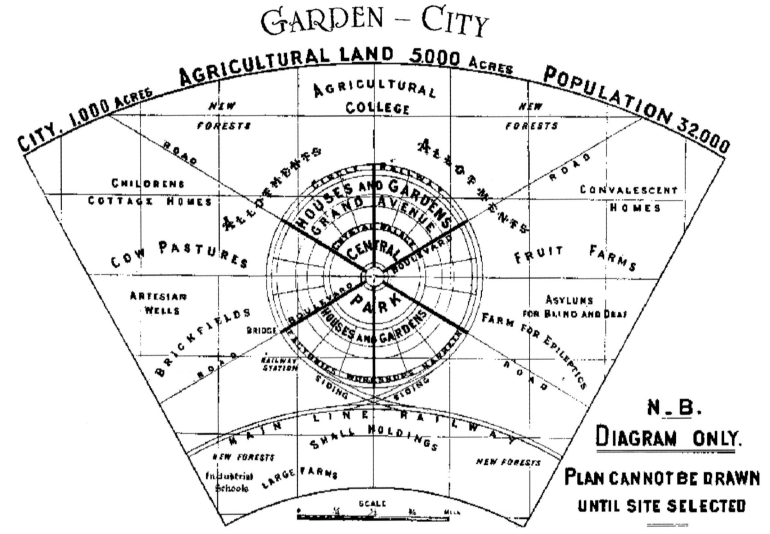

Figure 1.4 Ebenezer Howard's Garden City diagram.

catalyst for yet another Garden City. Subsequently, communities were planned that incorporated many of the Garden City ideas but at a larger scale. The British government formed the New Town Commission to manage the development of these larger new communities in England and Scotland. Milton Keynes, north of London, and Cumbernauld, in Scotland, were conceived under the auspices of the New Town Commission.

Community Design in America

During this same period of rapid industrialization (1850 to 1930), town planning in the United States took a slightly different turn.

Generally, the emphasis was more on the physical design elements of community than on an attempt to solve the social concerns that arose from the industrialization itself. In part, this focus was because industry leaders had not yet concerned themselves with the plight of their workers (a situation that would change with the union riots of 1877). Design leadership came from landscape architects intent on integrating the built environment and the land. The 1869 plan by Olmstead and Vaux for Riverside (Figure 1.5) brought this concept to life by blending roads and homes with the topography in a soft, garden-like setting.

Another contributing reason for the difference between British and American town

Credit: Courtesy of Robert C. Pusateri.

Figure 1.5 Riverside today.

planning was the source of funds for construction. British industrialists supported town planning through the building of company towns; development in the United States was primarily the result of land speculators building for a rapidly increasing population. Much of the growth in the United States was accommodated through the continued expansion of the urban grid. While functional, these neighborhoods had little character. At higher price ranges, however, design was important for two reasons. First, it gave the development a special character (art), resulting in a marketing advantage; second, it minimized development costs by working with the land and maximizing the number of buildable lots (science).

The Country Club (1911), in Kansas City, took the design of the neighborhood to a higher level by incorporating within the neighborhood a shopping district with wonderful amenities. Fountains adorn public spaces that are defined by delightful buildings (Figure 1.6), and graceful landscape accentuates residential lawns and intersections. The legacy of J.C. Nichols, whose vision built The Country Club, endures in the high value of each property in the district. Self-renewing deed restrictions, put in place to ensure continuation of the high standards established at the outset, control land use, setbacks, building projections, outdoor space, and signage. Like its British counterpart, Bournville, The Country Club District in Kansas City is a desirable place to live.

Following the First World War, many other development companies and the United States government created several new towns that have survived the test of time. Radburn, New Jersey (1928), and Chatham Village, in

Figure 1.6 A typical Country Club Plaza retail corner.

Pennsylvania (1932), are striking examples of private development that are still charming places to live. The US government, through the Suburban Resettlement Administration, focused on creating new towns for a broader range of incomes. Greendale in Wisconsin, Greenhills in Ohio, and Greenbelt near Washington, DC provided desperately needed housing in communities that were affordable for most families.

Unfortunately, the heavy demand for housing following the Second World War produced a dramatically different result. The sheer number of families being formed, and the availability of the Federal Housing Administration- and Veterans Administration-backed mortgages, created a need for modest housing quickly. The focus on speed and efficiency soon overshadowed more costly community-design considerations. The production building industry that emerged from this focus needed ever-increasing raw materials, including land, to keep the production line going. On the one hand, that the building industry met the needs of this country by supplying a large number of affordable homes in a short time is inspiring. On the other hand, that the industry has been slow to respond to criticism of the built environment and continues to build too many of the same thing is disappointing. *Sprawl*, as it is perceived today, is the image of the identical house stamped over and over again across the landscape.

In the early 1970s, *Planned Unit Developments (PUDs)* were believed to hold the answer to strict zoning standards and unimaginative planning. The thought was that each planned community could establish its own development and design standards to achieve a better design solution than the standard subdivision. The theory was that municipalities would approve variances in standards in exchange for a higher quality of design and implementation. In reality, getting approval for a PUD became time-consuming and expensive, and the standards that were approved were enforced without any flexibility or thought to changing

Timeline	
1813	Robert Owens establishes New Lanark, Scotland, which is the first company town
1853	Titus Salt establishes Saltaire, Yorkshire, England
1869	Olmstead and Vaux design Riverside, a Chicago suburb
1879	The Cadbury brothers (chocolate) establish Bournville
1887	The Lever brothers (soap) establish Port Sunlight
1894	George Cadbury expands Bournville, providing housing for people not employed at the chocolate factory
1902	Ebenezer Howard publishes "Garden Cities of Tomorrow"
1928	Radburn, New Jersey marks the beginning of the new town movement in the U.S.
1932	Chatham Village, Pennsylvania founded
1945	End of WWII generated significant demand for housing in the U.S. paid for by government backed financing and favorable tax laws
1970s	Planned Unit Development Ordinances are created to provide more flexibility than conventional zoning
1991	The Ahwahnee Principles are developed

market conditions. New ideas were difficult to implement and required a PUD amendment. Today, many communities approve only minor variations in standards, if any at all.

The Quality of Community

Community design, both good and bad, evolved from these early models. The experiences of the British and American town planners yield valuable lessons for today's community builder. In the United Kingdom, the attempts to enhance the quality of life for all income levels resulted in planning concepts that express useful relationships between open space, employment, and housing. Unfortunately, these concepts did not anticipate the impact of larger industries or the proliferation of the automobile. The rigid interpretation of the planning concepts at a larger scale has resulted in designs that fail to meet the aesthetic needs of the residents.

The following photograph illustrates how, at Cumbernauld, neighborhoods are defined by different materials and architectural styles (Figure 1.7). The gray and orange modular homes certainly met the needs of the low-income buyer, while, in an adjacent neighborhood, brick homes expressed a higher price

Figure 1.7 Lack of visual diversity within a low income neighborhood in Cumbernauld, Scotland.

and quality for a more affluent buyer. What both designs failed to understand is that visual diversity is necessary within each neighborhood. The symmetry of the low-income neighborhood was punctuated by parks that were overplanted and unusable. The richness of the brick was taken a step too far, with absolutely everything built out of brick. The neighborhood lost some of its appeal when the roads, sidewalks, landscape walls, and homes were all built of the same brick

In the United States, the early focus on the marriage of site and built environment resulted in visually beautiful places. The investment in community character and sense of place evident in several of the early communities continues to provide value to residents and to the builder whose reputation was enhanced by the work. A hard lesson still being learned by today's production builders is that the economies of scale resulting from the mass production of homes and lots will be tempered by the insistence of municipalities that community design be given greater consideration.

At its best, community design meets the needs of a diverse population through a variety of product types, sizes, and price ranges. The design is sensitive to the environment, respects the neighbors, and is a financial success. Thought is given to the events that happen and to the quality of the visual environment in the places that are designed. The community is sought after as a desirable place to live, and homes retain their values.

At its worst, housing is simply a commodity to be brought to market as cheaply as possible. Design is limited to the most efficient way to lay out streets and lots to minimize per-lot development costs and maximize lot yield,

while sacrificing the quality of the built environment. Architectural variety and common areas are eliminated as too costly to implement and maintain. Quality materials give way to square footage to gain an advantage on the product-comparison checklist. The home is sold as an isolated box, with little or no consideration given to the community in which it sits. Home values may appreciate with the rest of the market; however, they are often the first to depreciate in severe economic times.

The reality is that most developments fall somewhere in between these extremes. There are warning signs, however, of increasing pressure to move toward the idea of a home as a commodity. In 1974, the top 50 builders built 8.7 percent of the total single-family homes (Figure 1.8). Twenty-three years later, in 1997, the top 50 builders' share had increased to 16 percent, or more than 137,000 single-family homes.[1] These builders are dedicated to production methods with minimal flexibility in design or cost. Value is sold as the most house for the least money.

Many production builders rely on intermediary land developers for a portion of their lot supply. These speculative land developers often do not know at the early design stage who will be the final buyer for the development, and so the plans are made as generically and cheaply as possible to appeal to a wide range of potential production builders. Open spaces and amenities are ignored because they might increase the Home Owners Association dues, making the lot less competitive with other subdivisions. With this approach, to cre-

---

[1] "Concentration in Home Building," Gopal Ahluwalia, *Housing Economics*, December 1998.

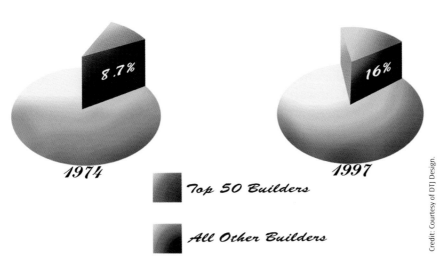

Market Share of the Top 50 Builders in the U.S. for Single Family

8.7%

16%

1974

1997

Top 50 Builders

All Other Builders

Credit: Courtesy of DTJ Design.

Figure 1.8 Comparison of the top 50 builders' market share in 1974 and 1997.

Speculative land developers purchase a parcel of land (or control it with a purchase contract contingent on rezoning), put together a team to create a subdivision design, obtain regulatory approvals, and develop the land for builders. It is not unusual for these developers to complete the approvals process before they identify a builder who will purchase finished lots. In order to appeal to a broad range of potential builder clients, and to keep costs low, speculative land developers want to maximize the number of lots, make the plan as generic as possible, and provide little, or no, common area.

ate a community that blends an unknown home to the land and meets the needs of an unidentified buyer is nearly impossible.

When the focus is limited to the house and coupled with the desire to reduce all costs to an absolute minimum, the builder/developer can be referred to as a *subdivider*. When the focus shifts to the character of the community, with a blending of the community design and architecture to the land, and an environmental sensitivity, the builder/developer can be referred to as a *community builder*. A community builder cares for the land, cares for the existing and future residents, and builds value for everyone. Community builders are usually visionaries and leaders in their communities.

Characteristics of Community

Several commonalities are found in all successful communities. Depending on the land and the market, these elements may be found in varying degrees, but they are usually present in some fashion. Attention to these elements is low in subdivisions and high in communities. They include

- sensitivity to the natural environment
- a reference to the history of the place
- a diversity of people
- social activities (Chapter 8)
- incomes (Chapter 8)
- product type (Chapter 8)
- spaces (Chapter 4 and Chapter 5)
- texture and color (Chapter 5)
- a recognizable character

- common themes expressed through architecture and landscape architecture
- compatibility with the neighborhood context

Sensitivity to the Natural Environment

Well-designed communities work with the land instead of fighting it. Sensitive natural areas such as steep slopes and wetlands become features of the plan. Natural vegetation is preserved as much as possible to enhance the value of future uses. Wildlife is respected, and consideration is given for the continuation or restoration of plant and animal habitats. Development systems are designed to minimize impact; roads are designed with topography to minimize *cut and fill* and site disturbance; storm-water systems are designed to cleanse runoff before it enters natural channels and water bodies; water and sewer systems use the latest technology to minimize disturbance.

Reference to the History of the Place

Well-designed communities reflect the historical and cultural heritage in which they are located. Development patterns, architectural styles, and amenities express how regions and localities developed. They link the cultural heritage of the people to the design of civic buildings and public spaces. Materials are indigenous to the region, and architectural design styles represent adaptations related to local climate and geography. At Pabst Farms, for example, this reference to the history of the place is evident in the community signage along Interstate 94 (Figure 1.9).

Diversity

Well-designed communities exhibit an understanding that stability is rooted in a celebration of diversity. A variety of housing types meets the needs of many income groups and lifestyle needs. The diversity allows people who work in the community to live in the community. A shared sense of purpose is gained when this diversity is mixed throughout neighborhoods, not segregated behind walls or security gates. Different housing types result in different architectural massing and details that enhance the visual quality of the community. Different people expect different amenities to respond to their lifestyles and ages. These amenities require different space sizes and designs. Together, the architectural and spatial diversity add texture and color to the community.

Recognizable Character

Well-designed communities exhibit a consistency of character. People know they are in a place different from its surroundings. Often, this character is the result of a subtle interplay of planning, architecture, and landscape architecture design (Figures 1.10, 1.11, and 1.12). Styles do not clash or compete with each other. Roadways have a special "feel" when one

---

Community Builder

A community builder is a builder or developer who is intent on creating a sense of community through community design elements, common open spaces, amenities and community programs. The purpose is to facilitate the social enjoyment of the residents.

A sense of place is created by the artful definition of space through the details of the physical environment, including massing and void, volume, color, texture, and materials, and human interaction within the space to create a memorable experience.

moves through the community. Pattern and scale of buildings are unique. The landscape is similar and ties various parts of the whole together. This recognizable character is referred to as "*sense of place.*"

Common Themes

Linked closely with recognizable character, common themes help define well-designed communities. Common themes are the major design ideas that bring a community together visually. Subtle variations on the theme are allowed as long as a common thread is maintained. A southern Wisconsin lake village is an example of a common theme articulated through design by the inclusion of elements typically found in such a village. These elements certainly include a strong relationship to the lake from public spaces, trails and roads, and fishing docks; a loose development pattern along the lake edge, transitioning to a more formal pattern further away; and even a small retail space anchored by a restaurant or tavern.

Compatibility with Neighborhood Context

Edges between well-designed communities and their neighbors are soft; there is a blending of character through land use, massing, color and

Credit: Courtesy of DTJ Design.

Figure 1.9 Pabst Farms community image sign along I-94.

texture, or adequate screening and buffering. Thought is given to improving the quality of the existing neighborhood through pedestrian and vehicular connectivity, shared amenities and open spaces, preservation of key view corridors, and increased diversity of housing opportunity.

Community builders increase the opportunity for success when they consider each element both individually and collectively in the design of their community. At times, compromises may be necessary to respond to the vagaries of the site, the market, and the competition; however, smart community builders find a way to balance community building with cost. They understand that by creating better neighborhoods today they will earn public recognition and enhance their reputation as community builders of tomorrow. This awareness will pay dividends in the approval process, will increase sales and values, and will result in timeless, delightful places.

Figure 1.10 McKay Landing 6-plex. Consistency of architectural styles help create a sense of place.

Figure 1.11 McKay Landing 4-plex. Consistency of architectural styles help create a sense of place.

Figure 1.12 McKay Landing SF. Consistency of architectural styles help create a sense of place.

CHAPTER 2
The Market

In North America, one measure of our quality of life is the choice we have in how we meet our need for shelter. For many, our relative affluence gives us the option to choose where and how we want to live based on our age and lifestyle preferences. We can live in apartments or single-family condominiums and transfer the burden of maintenance to others through a Home Owners Association; we can live in large, single-family detached homes so we can have big yards to raise a family; we can live in retirement communities and play golf with our friends; or we can live in the country for a taste of isolation or retreat. Understanding what buyers want is the first step to building a great community.

Major demographic indicators, including age, income, and familial status begin to suggest what a particular group of buyers may want with respect to the design of the community and the home. Individually, these groups are considered *market segments*, while the whole is simply referred to as "the market." A *residential market analysis* should be completed prior to, or concurrent with, the *initial site analysis*, which together form a foundation for community design. A competent market analysis is best performed by an organization or individual who combines the talents of:

- an experienced researcher
- someone who understand demographics
- a sociologist, someone who understands consumer behavior
- a visionary, someone who goes beyond rear-view-mirror statistical analysis to seek new trends and directions

The community designer plays an important role in the residential market analysis by helping to identify the link between the potential market and the site prior to finalizing a development program.

Residential Market Analysis

A *residential market analysis*, also referred to as a *market feasibility analysis*, determines whether there is enough demand for housing to support a proposed development. This analysis should be composed of three primary elements: an economic base analysis, an estimate of residential demand by housing type and price, and a summary of consumer preferences regarding site amenities and home features.

Market

For the purposes of this book, the market is defined as the total collection of people who are potential buyers or renters of housing. Market segments than are those people who share similar characteristics and may be inclined to purchase similar housing.

The *economic base analysis* documents the strength of the current, and future, regional and local economy as expressed through job growth by job type and income (Figure 2.1).

Residential demand follows as a result of the population and household growth required to fill new jobs, or from net births over deaths, and in migration (Figure 2.2).

Credit: Courtesy of DTJ Design.

Figure 2.1 New office buildings bring new jobs.

Figure 2.2 Housing starts respond to job creation.

Consumer preferences help community builders understand how important community and home features are for a buyer, and how much they are willing to pay for those features.

Together, these three elements tell builders the number of homes they will likely be able to build by type, size, and price range, and what amenities the home and community should include (Figure 2.3). The resulting development program guides the community designer in creating a successful community.

Economic Base Analysis

A good economic base analysis considers first the strength of the regional economy. Historical job growth is tracked and projected as modified by analysis of the major regional industries. Expansion or contraction by a major industry will have a ripple effect throughout the regional economy and must be understood. The type of industry also has a significant effect on the income associated with new job growth. As an example, given the amount of skill and training required for the biotech industry, a major expansion by a biotech company may result in the growth of high-income jobs. Conversely, expansion of a large recycling operation may result in the addition of lower-paid manual laborers. Both scenarios have a positive impact on job growth, but the resulting household growth, housing product, and price range will be significantly different. Each industry should be

Figure 2.3 Buyers' lifestyle choices have an impact upon community design.

analyzed individually, and an aggregate of the entire region should be completed.

The US Census provides much of the raw data needed to conduct an economic base analysis. Knowledgeable market researchers can glean information related to job and population growth by incomes and industry, both for the larger market area and the site-specific area. This information must be supplemented with local information, available from the local Chamber of Commerce, the Economic Development Agency, and even personal interviews with representatives of major regional employers. The combination of historical trends and local projections helps market researchers be more accurate in their predictions of future economic activity.

After the regional economy is analyzed, the impact must be translated to the vicinity of the project site. Local job growth by type and income must be determined. Higher-paid employees tend to live closer to their work, while lower-paid workers generally seek affordable housing wherever it may be. Some municipalities recognize these trends and actively try to promote more affordable housing in specific locations through their comprehensive policy plans. Regardless, site location will influence which market segment may be appropriate to target. Major industry expansion also results in additional service and support jobs to serve expanding company needs and the new employees migrating to the region. This job growth includes *direct service jobs* (biotech company employees, for example) and *indirect service jobs* (for example, grocery store employees). Direct-service job growth is usually located near the growth industry, while indirect-service job growth is usually located in areas where new employees live. These jobs need to be considered when developing a program for the site.

New jobs generally result in household growth as new people and families move into the region to fill vacant positions. The nature of the household is somewhat dependent on the type of job created and the income associated with that job. These factors affect the type and price of housing required to meet the needs of the new household. As an example, the emerging high-tech industry of the late 1990s attracted young, highly educated singles and young couples. These individuals often worked long hours and reaped significant monetary rewards. By virtue of the relatively small family unit (single or couple), growth in this industry resulted in the creation of a large number of households and a demand for high-end, maintenance-free living. This demand was met through the development of expensive patio homes, or of somewhat less-expensive but still high-end condominiums. The market study should predict what type of household growth is expected as a result of job growth.

Household growth is also influenced by the age of the regional population, changes in familial situations, and the net impact on population growth of births, deaths, and migration. Children leaving home create new households. Divorces create two households from one. People moving into or out of the region need a place to live, or they leave a place for another to live. Population trends should

be tracked and evaluated to identify opportunities in the marketplace. Once the economics of the region and site have been assessed by employment, population, and household growth, attention must turn to the correlation of this growth to the demand for homes by type and price.

Residential Demand

The primary purpose of the residential demand analysis is to balance the supply of new homes by type and price to the need generated by household growth. The first step is to determine what type of housing product best serves the needs of each identified market segment. An analysis of past growth by industry and historical building-permit information reveals how similar growth was accommodated. This information is reviewed within the context of current market expectations and an appreciation for subtle differences in attitudes. For example, historical data indicated that many active adults desired to live in a maintenance-free environment, often as a second home in a retirement community located in a warmer climate. Today, this same market segment still wants the maintenance-free lifestyle associated with patio homes, but many prefer to stay near the community in which they reside, to enjoy the comfort of familiar surroundings and friends. To fill this need, primary-home, active-adult communities now exist in many major northern metropolitan areas.

Figure 2.4 suggests general correlations between market segments and product type:

One amenity that appears to span all market segments is a desire for more walkable communities. This feature may represent a

Market segment	Characteristics	Product type	Amenities
Young singles	Lower income/price and location sensitive	Apartments, can be either urban or suburban setting, price is more important than location	Active retail/recreation
Young singles	Higher income	Apartments/condominiums, can be either an urban or suburban setting, however, higher densities may be found in urban settings	Active retail/onsite recreation
Mature singles	Higher income/home as an investment	Apartments/condominiums/town homes, can be either an urban or suburban setting	Maintenance free living/close to work/quality design and finish
Young couple	First-time buyer, price sensitive	Town homes/small lot single family, location is not as important as price	Limited yard/open space/value space
Mature couple, no kids	High income/often dual income	Town home/condominium/cluster single family/estate single family, can be either an urban or suburban setting, second home/ vacation markets may be a possibility	Quality design and finish/close to shopping and restaurants/no-maintenance living
Young family	1st time move-up buyer	Single family/cluster single family, usually a suburban setting	Close proximity to schools, shopping, open space and recreation are a must/value space
Mature family	2nd time move-up buyer	Single family/luxury single family, usually a suburban setting, second home/vacation home market may be a possibility	Proximity to schools, shopping and recreation and quality of design and finish
Single parent		Town home/condominium/small lot single family/patio home, usually a suburban setting	Maintenance free living/security
Empty nester/ active adult	High disposable income	Patio homes/town homes/luxury single family/estate homes, can be either an urban or suburban setting, second home/vacation home may be a possibility	Quality design and finish/open spaces and cultural activities

Figure 2.4 Market segments vs. product type.

desire for a greater "connectedness" between residents or for a finer texture of open spaces within a community. It may relate to a historical image of what community should be. Whatever the reason, community design should reflect this desire. There need to be places to go, and trails and sidewalks on which to walk.

The second step is to determine the net demand for housing. Doing this requires that the demand for new housing, by type and price, must be reduced by the existing and proposed supply of housing. An analysis of completed for-sale homes, and homes under construction in the market, must be considered. A summary of all competing projects should be completed to inventory location, number, type, and price of homes available within the site market area. This inventory should also consider special site features and amenities that may give a project a competitive advantage. Potentially competing projects that are still in the planning stages must also be inventoried. Each project should be analyzed to determine its impact on the site and market. Existing and planned projects may meet the needs of an entire market segment, suggesting that an alternative development strategy is necessary.

Niche Markets

Gaps in supply and demand, or very small demand in specific market segments, may indicate an opportunity to fill a niche market with a targeted housing product. Overlooked *infill* parcels, small or irregular-shaped parcels, or parcels with unique site features may also be appropriate for niche markets. The opportunity lies in the fact that larger, production-oriented builders tend not to develop special product for a small market segment or make sufficient profits on more irregular lots. Their production systems are set up to minimize customization of any building or development component. They require the efficiencies of building the same thing many times.

A builder who has designed a production system to accommodate changes by the buyer, or who has the organizational and financial flexibility to respond quickly to changing market conditions, may be able to take advantage of niche opportunities. A niche builder should reexamine properties that have been overlooked in the past, understand why they have been neglected, and determine whether market conditions are favorable enough to mitigate the past concerns. Niche builders must also be able to stay in touch with the desires and expectations of various market segments and be able to transition from building one housing type to another with ease.

Finally, it is also important to consider the number of resale homes and apartment vacancies in the market. These may absorb some of the demand created by job or population growth and reduce the market for new homes. In March 2003, *Builder* magazine reported that 80 percent of homes sold are previously owned homes, while only 20 percent are new homes. Previously owned homes represent significant competition in the market and usually offer a wide variety of housing choice.

The result of these three steps is a summary of the number of homes by product type, price range, and size needed to meet the needs of the identified market. The summary should

Many Americans want to be part of a community and not just have a place to live. Building community responds to that need.

include the expected density and the annual and total acreage needed for each product type.

Consumer Preferences

Providing the features and amenities that the buyer wants in the community and the home gives designers and builders a competitive advantage in the marketplace. Within the home, these features include unit size, number of bedrooms, number of baths, special features in the kitchen or bath, and number and type of other rooms. Outside the home, amenities could include open spaces and trails, lakes, active play areas, golf courses or other recreational options, convenience neighborhood retail, community buildings, and community programs. In 1999, American LIVES, Inc., a market-research firm located in Oakland, California, published a study that explored what buyers said they wanted in their communities. This study was based on a national sample that, through various statistical analyses, determined major trends in buyer preferences.

Significant for community builders, the overwhelming response in this study favored natural areas, smaller parks, and green spaces as the most desired amenity. This desire for open space included trails, biking paths, and sidewalks. Gathering places and town centers within the community were also a high priority. Interestingly, golf courses and gated neighborhoods were far down the list, appealing to only a small segment of the market. The study did confirm that many Americans want to be part of a community and not just have a place to live. Building community responds to that need.

This kind of information is often available from national research firms and can be fine-tuned to your market by exit interviews, focus groups, and/or buyer surveys.

- *Exit interviews.* Conducted by third-party research groups who ask potential buyers leaving model home complexes what they like or dislike in the model homes and/or the community.
- *Focus groups.* Imminent buyers with similar characteristics to the identified market. They are shown pictures of alternate features and amenities and asked to rank the importance of a feature, and generally how much they would be willing to pay for the feature.
- *Buyer surveys.* Discover why recent buyers purchased the home they are in. They also indicate what the buyers would change after they have been in the house for a while. These surveys are valuable in that they represent recent decisions made by real buyers.

Some builders rely more on intuition than research in creating a development program for their site. They listen to the advice of real estate agents, or they simply reflect on the past successes or failures of their work. Although this information is valuable and can be visionary, confirming these assumptions with objective analysis is important. Market analysis can reduce the risks inherent in community development and may also facilitate financing by increasing lender confidence.

Understanding Housing Types

As one of the main elements in community design, the quality of residential architecture has a tremendous impact on the success of a community. Quality architecture begins with an assimilation of the building program, as defined by the market study; the exterior composition and character of the building to support the community vision; and the building's relationship to adjacent structures because they contribute to the texture of the neighborhood. Size and organization of rooms; views into, through, and out of the building to outdoor spaces; volume; texture; and details are all important elements of the building that must be considered within the context of the building and the community. As these spaces are designed, the exterior *massing*, detail, color, and texture bring the building to life.

There are many types of residential buildings on different kinds of lots, each responding to a particular market segment. Differences occur in the type of ownership and in how individual units are put on a lot or together in a building. Ownership is generally broken into the following two types:

- *Fee simple ownership.* The home or unit is sold with an individually described lot.
- *Condominium ownership.* The building is sold along with others, and the land under the unit or units is undivided and owned in common by all of the unit owners. This arrangement most often takes the form of stacked units. *Town-homes* are usually two-story, attached units sold as fee simple ownership.

Single-family condominiums are single-family detached units sold with a common interest in the land.

Quality community design builds on an understanding of the various building and lot types, what markets they serve, and generally what land forms work best for each building type. Ideally, to take advantage of site amenities, views, topography, and access, the community and architectural design are developed together. Building design can reinforce the community character, frame views, accentuate outdoor spaces, screen undesirable views, and provide texture along the street.

Detached single-family homes are the most common form of home ownership in the United States. Since 1976, with the exception of only five years, at least one million single-family homes have been sold in the United States each year. Many people think of a detached single-family home on a large lot as the epitome of the American Dream. In some respects, this ideal is changing. Buyers today seek more from their community than just a house on a street. People are looking for neighborhood amenities within walking distance, gathering places, a more refined street scene, and an opportunity to stay in their community even as their housing needs change. Buyers are not settling for less; they are purchasing the home that responds to their individual housing needs.

Demographic shifts associated with the aging of the Baby Boomers suggest that single-family housing will be increasing at a slower rate in the years to come. Recent studies (AmericanLIVES, 1999, NAHB Smart Growth 1999) suggest that as people age and their

Market analysis can reduce the risks inherent in community development and may also facilitate financing by increasing lender confidence.

children move from home, a growing percentage desire to live in a denser, fully maintained environment close to shopping and cultural activities. Without considering housing diversification, single-family builders may find themselves competing for fewer buyers.

Detached Single-Family Housing

Within this category, there are many different types of lots and home designs. Single-family detached lots accommodate both single-level ranch units or two-story units. Either configuration may have a walk-out basement, which increases the amount of livable square footage and the value of the home. Most lot sizes relate to the width of the unit, which is typically a function of the size and number of rooms within the home. Mixing lot and product type can increase the potential market for the community and will enhance the visual diversity.

Estate Lots

Usually, lots more than an acre in size (43,560 sq. ft.) are considered an *estate lot*. Estate lots may range from 1 acre to more than 35 acres in size. Because they consume large amounts of land, estate lots contribute to sprawl; however, they appeal to people who desire relative isolation or a sense of retreat. Most estate lots in suburban areas are expensive due to the large amount of land devoted to a single home. Buyers expect a greater sense of individuality and privacy with estate lots. Creating *building envelopes* and *view corridors* in the site plan helps to achieve these expectations.

Given the high expectations of the estate home buyer, land with special or unique char-acteristics is most appropriate for this housing product. Wonderful views, water, interesting topography, and significant vegetation are natural amenities that create an opportunity for higher-priced, estate lots (Figure 2.5). To fully realize the potential of the land, one must sometimes consider the necessity to minimize disturbance of the natural features that make the site special. Selective clearing, retaining walls, tree-preservation techniques, preservation of key site features, view corridors, building envelopes, no-clear zones, alternate road standards, and custom home design are several strategies that can retain high land values.

Half-Acre Lots

Half-acre lots are often the minimum lot size that county health departments will allow for septic sewer treatment. Some jurisdictions consider 20,000-square-foot lots to be ½-acre lots. The difficulty with ½-acre lots is that they are too big to create a sense of community by clustering buildings and too small to meet the expectations of the estate-lot buyer. Unless well planned and landscaped, homes on these lots tend to look lost.

For land with public services, most landforms are appropriate for ½-acre lots; however, special care is necessary to preserve natural features. Because the lots are too small to preserve natural features on individual lots, special areas should be identified and held in common (Figure 2.6). Doing this will reduce the number of lots, yet net values will remain high as a result of the added premiums for natural features. Land without public services is limited by regulations related to the design of septic systems. Poor soils and steep slopes

Figure 2.5 A well-designed estate home capitalizes on its surroundings.

make septic systems too expensive or inappropriate.

10,000-Square-Foot Lots

In many communities, 10,000-square-foot lots (considered ¼-acre lots in some locations) are now thought of as luxury home lots. These lots and homes appeal to second- and third-time, move-up buyers with children, and space is seen as a necessity.

Gross densities are approximately 3 homes per acre (development units/acre, or du/ac). Typical dimensions are 90 feet by 120 feet, with 10-foot to 12-foot side yards. This lot width allows for a three-car, front-loaded garage with more than half of the front eleva-

tion non-garage. The front elevation can be improved with *alternative-loaded*—either *back-* or *side-loaded*—garages. The importance of the alternate-loaded garage is to ensure that the architecture of the home is visually more important than the garage.

Homes built on 10,000-square-foot lots work best on land that has less than a 12 percent slope. The wider side-yard setbacks allow for street grades of up to 8 percent without the need for significant site walls between buildings. Walkout units, alternately loaded garages, garages that move up or down in relation to the home's finished floor elevation, and roads that generally parallel the slope are strategies to reduce site-development costs. Wider lots on

Figure 2.6 Clustering home sites preserves many of the sites' unique features.

the uphill side of roads allow for driveways to access side-loaded garages at a higher elevation to minimize the need for *tuck-under* garages. Land with more than a 12 percent slope increases site development cost through the need for more site walls, extended foundations, and extensive grading.

Less-than-10,000-square-foot lots are typically referred to by width. The lot sizes relate to the width of the home coupled with the appropriate setbacks. Builders usually build homes in 2-foot increments to save on standard material sizes. For lot widths between 55 feet and 90 feet, side-yard setbacks are often between 7.5 feet and 12 feet. As the lots get narrower, the garages become more dominant. Developing design strategies to minimize the negative impact of the garage is important. Again, back- (a minimum of 4 feet) or side-loaded garages help improve the street scene. For many buyers, expectations include a three-car garage with each home. As lot width decreases, reducing the number of garages provided with each unit, or looking to alley-loaded configurations, may be necessary. Lots between 60 feet and 90 feet wide typically achieve gross densities between 3 du/ac and 4 du/ac.

These lot widths accommodate both ranch and two-story home designs; single-story plans become limited in size as the lot becomes smaller. The smaller-lot homes appeal to first-time, move-up buyers, while the larger lots appeal to larger families or second-time, move-up buyers. Today, a majority of homes is built on these lot types. In the future, as household formation changes due to changing demographics, other housing products may become more appropriate to respond to different needs.

Given the smaller side-yard setbacks, these homes should be built on land with less than 8 percent slope. Road grades generally cannot exceed 6 percent without special architectural design considerations or site walls between buildings. Useable yard space is considered a necessary lot feature that limits the amount of grading that can occur between buildings. Walkout units can accommodate some grade change; however, the three-story rear elevations can visually overpower small rear yards (Figure 2.7).

Small Lots

Lots less than 50 feet wide are referred to as small lots. They are usually 100 feet to 110 feet deep and have shallower front and rear setbacks than larger single-family lots. Front yard setbacks may be as little as 12 feet, and rear yard setbacks might be as small as 10 feet. Side yard setbacks may be as little as 5 feet. At least 25 percent of the garages on the street should be alternative loaded because 50 percent or more of the front elevation on a typical front-loaded, small-lot house is garage door. In addition to the back- and side-loaded garage alternatives, various court clusters or alley-loaded configurations are often used to minimize the negative visual impact of the garage. Various configurations of small lots can reach densities of up to 7 du/ac on narrow public streets or private drives. Small lots are generally lower priced as a result of the amortization of land and development costs over a greater number of units. These homes appeal to both the first-time buyer and the move-down buyer who simply needs less home than before and prefers a maintenance-free lifestyle.

Figure 2.7 Three-story walkouts can be visually overpowering.

As lots become smaller, it is important that the architecture of the unit be designed as part of the lot layout. The amount of outdoor space on each lot becomes smaller as the lots become smaller. Narrow side yards between buildings become unusable for both property owners. As a result, it is necessary to design the home to effectively use as much of the lot as possible.

One solution is to create a *zero-lot-line home,* in which one side of the house has a zero setback, while the other side has the full setback between buildings. This configuration allows each home to have full use of the space between buildings. The architecture of the house is developed to take advantage of the additional space at the side of the home. Inte-

rior courts can become the focal point for each room facing the court, and each can have an access onto the court. Unfortunately, most jurisdictions do not allow windows on the zero-setback side of the home, and all will require some type of maintenance easement to allow the homeowner to maintain the zero-setback side.

To mitigate these problems, some communities allow for a typical side-yard setback, with a use easement for one side given to the adjacent property. Building codes allow window penetrations, and the homeowner has the capability to maintain the property. The adjacent homeowner also has the capability to use the easement area of the neighbor's lot and can improve it with landscape and *hardscape*. This type of lot configuration works well with small-lot cluster design.

A variety of cluster designs can be used to meet the density needs of this market segment. Higher densities reduce the land and site-development cost per unit, resulting in a more affordable home. *Pinwheel clusters, motor courts, stub streets, eyebrows, alley-loaded streets* and *court clusters* (Figures 2.8, 2.9, and 2.10) all provide higher-density solutions while providing visual diversity. A variety of solutions should be used to eliminate the monotony of too much of the same thing.

Small-lot, single-family homes are most appropriate for relatively flat sites (less than 6 percent slope). The limited amount of open space between buildings on these lots makes site grading and drainage more difficult and

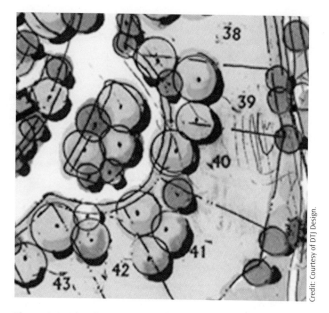

Credit: Courtesy of DTJ Design.

Figure 2.9 A landscape "eyebrow."

expensive. To minimize site walls between buildings, roads should not exceed 4 percent slope. Although walkout units can be built on steeper slopes, uphill lots are difficult to build on without special architectural design solutions. Some solutions, such as tuck-under garages, may have a negative impact on the visual quality of the street and can be difficult

Walkout Units

Walkout units have a lower level that has direct, at grade access on the side, or rear of the home. The main level has direct, at grade access at the front of the home. Walkout units generally sell for more than non-walkout units since there is the opportunity for more inviting living spaces on the lower level.

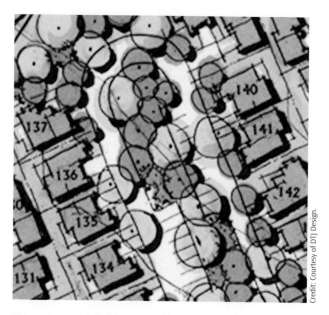

Credit: Courtesy of DTJ Design.

Figure 2.8 A small auto court with internal parking.

Figure 2.10 A hammerhead court.

to market. Special site features should be pre-served in common areas, and clusters should be designed to maximize access or views.

Urban Cottages

With the advent of *traditional neighborhood development (TND)*, there has been a renewed interest in small, *urban-style cottages*. The homes are typically alley accessed with small yards. Urban cottages appeal to young singles, couples with no children, and empty-nester buyers. They rely on the urban fabric to provide suitable amenities, and parks must be within easy walking distance. A mix of housing types and supporting retail and cultural facilities are desired community features. This housing type is often built in urban infill areas

within close proximity to the required amenities.

As lots and homes become smaller, the desirable characteristics that buyers find important in single-family homes are more difficult to achieve (Figure 2.11). These features include a sense of individuality, privacy, and useable outdoor spaces. A *density threshold* is reached when these characteristics diminish so much that the buyer no longer perceives their benefit. Reaching this threshold suggests that a new product type is necessary to meet the needs of the market. Depending on local perceptions, the density threshold varies. As detached single-family homes lose the desired characteristics, attached single-family homes may be more appropriate.

Figure 2.11 Loss of privacy and usable space occurs when yards get too small.

Attached Single-Family Homes

This category refers to fee simple for-sale homes that share one or two common walls with the adjacent home. Attached garages, with direct access to the home, are expected. These homes include townhomes and *twin homes* (*duplexes*).

Townhomes are attached single-family units commonly composed in buildings of 3 to 8 units per building. Generally, when buildings are more than 8 units, they become too large to be workable in a community site design.

Twin homes (duplex units) will often achieve 7 du/ac, while townhomes can achieve densities of between 8 du/ac and 10 du/ac. More than 10 du/ac townhomes need to be sited in a more formal pattern, and then take on the characteristics of an urban row home.

Many of the benefits of larger-lot, detached single-family homes can be achieved in a duplex unit, while increasing density. Increasing density can make the home more affordable or help pay for landscaping and amenities. Outdoor private spaces, separate entries and garages, and even the look of a single-family detached home can be achieved with duplex units (Figure 2.12). Access to the building and garage can be designed to reinforce the perception of living in a detached single-family home. Because there are no interior units, it is possible to provide windows and light on three sides of the home. This benefit results in higher building values than those of townhomes with more attached units.

An attached single-family home can either be placed on a fee simple lot or designed as a condominium. If it is designed as a condominium, the owner still owns the land under the unit but owns the remaining land as an undivided interest. One benefit of condominium ownership is the full-service mainte-

Credit: Courtesy of DTJ Design.

Figure 2.12 Duplex units can be designed to look like a large, single-family home.

nance of the exterior of the home and the grounds. This advantage appeals to market segments that may not have the time or the inclination to perform home maintenance. The condominium design might be in a second-home market in which people live in the home only part of the year, or in a market of active singles or couples, in which people spend more time at work and recreation and less time at home.

Other forms of attached single-family condominiums include *manor homes* and *combination buildings* composed of townhomes and stacked condominiums. Manor homes are multiple-unit buildings designed to give the appearance of a large, single-family home. They have a similar scale as traditional single-family homes and many of the architectural features (porches, pop-outs) that are identified with detached single-family homes. They can be used to increase affordability through higher density, or as a transitional option between single-family homes and traditional

multifamily buildings. Likewise, combination buildings often give the appearance of a large, single-family building or a traditional town-home building (Figure 2.13). This building type is used to increase density in order to increase affordability. Manor homes can achieve densities of up to 12 du/ac, while combo buildings can achieve densities up to 20 du/ac.

At higher price ranges and densities, attached single-family homes can allow luxurious landscaped settings, which result in high-quality visual impact within the community. The focus is often on common areas between buildings; intimate landscaped spaces; plazas; or even active amenities such as pools, community buildings, or tennis courts. Common-area maintenance ensures that the landscaped areas will continue to provide value for the entire community. Including attached single-family homes in the community can improve the overall visual quality of a community, increase density to amortize site-development

Credit: Courtesy of DTJ Design.

Figure 2.13 A manor home takes on the characteristics of a single-family home.

costs (making homes more affordable or helping to pay for site amenities), and appeal to a broader market. As a component of the development program, attached single-family homes increase market absorption through product segmentation and housing variety. Together, these benefits can increase sales pace and home values.

Single-family attached buildings can be built on a variety of slopes. The buildings are often designed to accommodate grade changes through lower-level walkouts. One limiting factor is the organization of garages. Garages too close together reduce the capability of the building to take up grade along the length of the building, and stepping between units is expensive. As a result, larger townhome buildings must be sited strictly parallel to the slope. This requirement creates the need to design uphill units, which are often more difficult to sell.

Alternatives are to design smaller buildings, buildings in which garages are separated enough to allow a step between units (which can improve the visual quality of the building by breaking up the roof massing), or garage clusters that allow for one driveway access to the street for several garages. Without architectural solutions, massive grading might be necessary to eliminate uphill units. This approach can have a negative impact on natural site features and will likely increase costs.

Multifamily Housing
Multifamily housing refers to a collection of individual units that are attached on the side and/or top or bottom. Because many of the units occupy only air space, these buildings are usually sold as condominium ownership, or are not sold but rented as apartments. Depending on the building configuration and unit sizes, multifamily buildings often achieve densities between 12 du/ac and 25 du/ac. Buildings with more than 25 du/ac are typically over three stories high and require elevators. Higher-density buildings are most often found in large, urban settings. *Stacked flats*, or single-level living units on top of each other, and *three-story walkups* are the most prevalent type of multifamily buildings.

At higher densities, providing attached garages with direct access to the home is difficult. Multiple stairs or expensive hallways are architectural solutions to this problem. Single-car garages with direct access, or detached garages, are alternatives. Carriage units over detached garages represent one strategy to provide the necessary garage parking in a building that blends visually with the rest of the community. It is important to mitigate the poor visual quality of many garage doors in close proximity. Building elements cantilevered over garage doors, horizontal breaks in garage facades, planting areas along garage facades, and high-quality garage door designs can help.

In an urban setting, multifamily buildings can take on the character and form of row homes with reduced front setbacks and less yard space. The reduced unit open space should be offset with small pocket parks and green spaces along the street. More attention to the design of the building and higher-quality materials are also necessary to enhance the visual quality of the street. To minimize the negative impact of the garages, alleys should be kept short and should not allow views from one public street to another.

Site grading can also be a challenge with large multifamily buildings. The number of attached garages, or the proximity of detached garages, requires large, flat building pads. If slopes are more than 3 percent to 4 percent, large retaining walls or slope areas may be necessary to accommodate the building and parking. These designs can disturb natural features, increase site development costs through walls or massive grading, or reduce density. Smaller buildings can be more sensitively sited; however, this approach will result in lower densities.

Architectural Design Strategies

To respond to changing market conditions, architectural design must be flexible to allow a variety of design features. Common to many homes are flex options that allow the buyer to choose from a variety of room alternatives that meet their specific needs. These might include a den/bedroom option, expanded master suites, or playrooms over the garage. Designing different homes that fit on the same foundation might be necessary to change the design completely.

One recent trend is the option to move a garage to respond to front-load, side-load, or alley-load lot conditions. This option allows for essentially the same house to fit on a variety of lot types within the same community, or provides a different look for the same house. Either way, it creates visual diversity within the community and responds to different buyer preferences. Variations in roof massing, materials, and elevation styles add even more visual interest. The graphic in Figure 2.14 illustrates

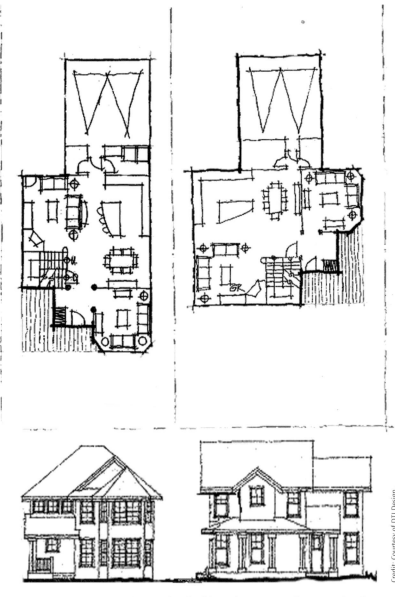

Figure 2.14 The same footprint can be sited in various ways to increase visual diversity.

Credit: Courtesy of DTJ Design.

that creating visual interest is possible without requiring different floor plans.

Flexibility in multifamily buildings is more difficult due to the size and complexity of the buildings. A solution to this problem is to create interchangeable modules that fit within each building. In one building, for example, two stacked flats occupy the designated space; in another building, a stacked flat is under a two-story condominium in the same space; in a third building, a commercial space is under a stacked flat (Figure 2.15). If stacked flats are selling better, then the building can be put together with more stacked-flat modules, while the same flexibility is available if townhomes or retail space is more desirable. These plans can accommodate a live/work arrangement in which the street level may start out as a rental unit and be converted to a storefront or office in the future.

Housing Diversity

Given the variety of housing opportunity and choice, there should be a place for everyone in the community. Communities are strengthened by a diversity of incomes and lifestyles. They are more resilient to economic changes, and their value appreciates more rapidly. Policemen, firemen, and teachers can live in the communities they serve. As their lives change, people can move within the neighborhood instead of away from the community. Housing diversity increases absorption by appealing to a larger market, and it can reduce amortized costs faster. Housing diversity also adds to the texture of the community. Quality of life is influenced by how neighborhoods and communities are organized.

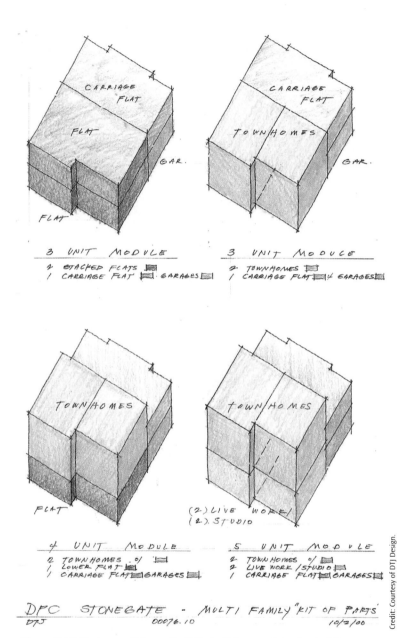

Figure 2.15 Various unit types that fit a building module give builders flexibility to respond to changing markets.

CHAPTER 3
Understanding Site Context

Quality community design is in part a response to, and a reflection of, the environmental and man-made influences of the site and its context. The physical opportunities and constraints of soils, slopes, hydrology, geology, climate, vegetation, views, noise, and wildlife should guide the community design in a manner that respects natural systems. Working with the land protects environmental features, which enhances the value of the community and minimizes development costs. The community theme and design concept should evolve from an understanding of the site's physical characteristics and the climate and environment of the region. Environmental features should be integrated into the community design and celebrated by providing views and access to these features. People appreciate this connection to the land and will often pay more for communities that exhibit these features.

Man-made infrastructure (including roads and access, water and sewer systems, natural-gas distribution systems, electric, cable, and telephone lines) and the cultural influences of land use (development regulations, historical or archeological assets, and community perceptions and values) also have an impact on the quality of the built environment. At times, engineering considerations may limit community design flexibility, while ease of maintenance and fear of liability cause some communities to ignore new design ideas. The community designer must understand all of the infrastructure systems and development standards, to balance the physical requirements of development with the quality-of-life needs of the residents.

Environmental Assessment

Although a detailed understanding of each of the environmental influences is critical to quality community design, these factors also must be considered collectively as an eco-system, whereby modification of one element has significant and lasting impact on another. For example, simple road grading can remove ground cover while concentrating run-off, resulting in erosion and loss of soil, which increase the silt in an adjacent stream; this in turn causes damage to the aquatic habitat. Mitigating impacts is usually more expensive than minimizing impacts in the first place. One method to minimize impacts is to do a *sensitivity analysis* for each environmental influence, all then overlaid to form a composite map of environmentally sensitive and developable areas.

This process, described by Ian McHarg in his book *Design with Nature*, begins with an inventory of each environmental element and an analysis of its sensitivity to change. For example, soils with high expansion coefficients or high erosion potential would be classified as severe limitations for development. Another map might illustrate surface water, regulated wetland areas, and high subsurface water table as severe limitations for development. A *slope map* might show areas of little limitation, moderate limitation, and severe limitation for development. When this data is combined, those areas that are severe on all maps suggest that no development should take place, while areas with one severe limitation or moderate limitations might be developed with an understanding of the mitigation required for development. The composite also will identify those areas that are suitable for development with little or no environmental mitigation required.

Today, *geographical information systems (GISs)* make gathering and analyzing information faster and easier. A GIS is a computer-based mapping system (Figure 3.1) that allows the user to manipulate criteria and determine multiple impacts. Many larger municipalities have invested significant time and energy to create GIS mapping for both natural and man-made systems within their boundaries. Often, this information is available to the community builder, and planning departments will use the information to evaluate the impact of a proposed community plan. The example below illustrates how GIS mapping can help formulate the appropriate location for a new mountain community in Colorado.

In addition to an analysis of development suitability, an understanding of what features and elements present opportunities to enhance the value of the community is necessary. Many

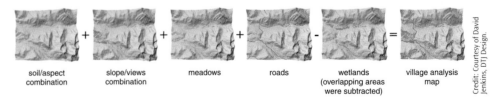

soil/aspect combination + slope/views combination + meadows + roads − wetlands (overlapping areas were subtracted) = village analysis map

Credit: Courtesy of David Jenkins, DTJ Design.

Figure 3.1 A series of GIS overlay maps can quickly and accurately reveal appropriate development areas.

of the elements that are identified as being unsuitable for development can be weaved into the design of the community. At Meadow Sweet Farm, in Erie, Colorado, for example (Figures 3.2 and 3.3), a stand of large cottonwood trees and a natural drainage area were considered inappropriate for development and instead became primary elements in the open space and trail system running throughout the community. The trees anchor a large park at the top of the hill, and the trail along the drainage corridor provides pedestrian access to the school, parks, and adjacent housing. Views across the park to the mountains significantly increase the value for homes within the neighborhood and for the existing neighborhood to the east.

Soils

Some soils have a tremendous impact on community development. Although many negative impacts can be overcome, doing so is often time-consuming and expensive. The most common problems with soils relate to their expansiveness, erosion potential, and structural integrity. In locations without sewer service, where there is a reliance on septic systems to provide proper sewage disposal, *permeability* of the soil will have an impact on development. With too much permeability (the rate at which water moves through the soil), contamination of the ground water is a possibility, while too little permeability causes the *effluent* to back up in the system, eliminating the soil's natural ability to break down the effluent into harmless natural compounds.

Expansive soils are typically fine clays that have very small particles. As water enters the soil, it binds to the surface of the particles,

increasing their relative size and causing the soil to expand. Expanding soils can heave roads and building foundations, creating unsafe conditions (Figure 3.4). In more serious cases, water and sewer lines can break, and walls can separate. Designing special foundations and controlling water during and after development are necessary to limit potential damage. Structural basement floors, piers, and grade beams, over-excavation, and water treatment are a few of the techniques used to mitigate expansive soils. Once the property is developed, proper drainage away from buildings and roads is important to minimize long-term damage

Erosion potential of soils becomes more critical as slope increases. As the slope increases, the velocity of water moving across the land increases. This, combined with the impact of rain on the soil, dislodges soil particles, allowing them to be carried downstream (Figure 3.5). Erosion can quickly damage roads and building foundations, make open land unusable, and damage aquatic habitat. The best methods to minimize erosion are to limit the amount of development on steeper slopes, minimize the disturbance of any existing protective ground cover, and reestablish vegetation rapidly. Narrow street sections that reduce cut and fill, and no-disturbance zones on lots are two proven methods to reduce the amount of erosion.

Poor structural qualities in soils are difficult to overcome. They might become fluid when wet or they might collapse under the weight of buildings or roads. Retaining walls may be needed to hold up even shallow slopes. Trees may blow over in gentle winds. It is often necessary to import better soil, or sand and

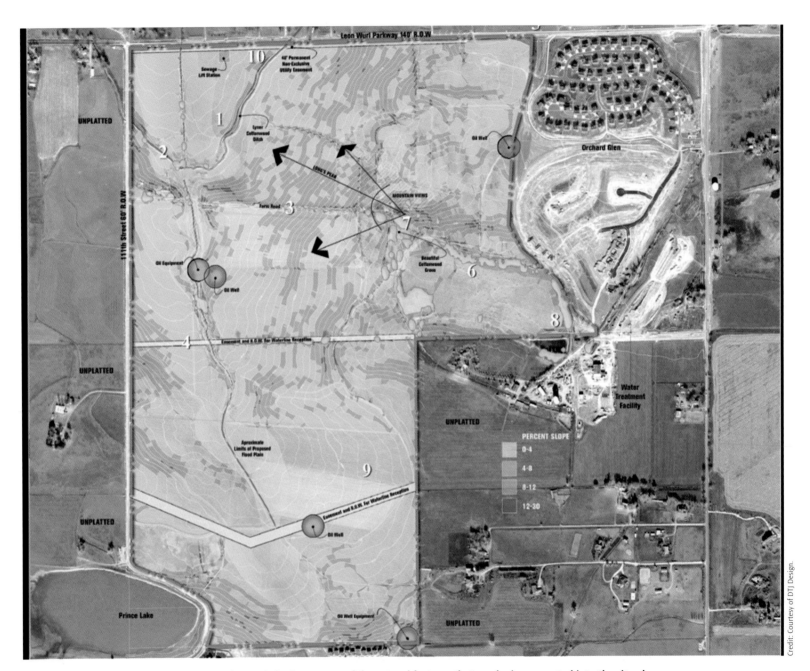

Figure 3.2 A portion of the Meadow Sweet site analysis shows some of the natural features that can be incorporated into the site plan.

Credit: Courtesy of DTJ Design.

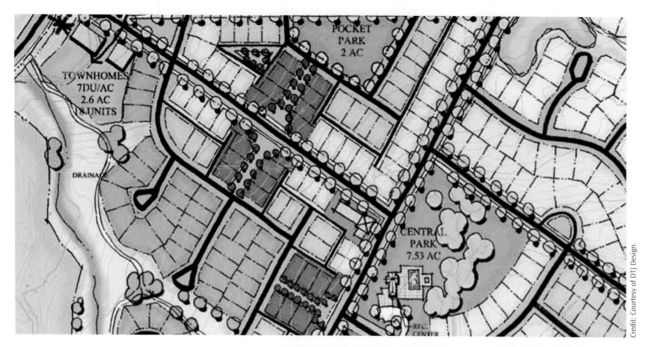

Credit: Courtesy of DTJ Design.

Figure 3.3 The Meadow Sweet site plan illustrates how natural features can become part of the community amenities.

Figure 3.4 A heaving sidewalk is an indication of highly expansive soils that have not been properly mitigated.

Figure 3.5 An unprotected fill slope can quickly erode, causing downstream damage.

gravel, to create a solid base for roads and buildings. Unless other site features outweigh these negatives, it is best to avoid poor structural soils entirely. The soil profile, (Figure 3.6) or cross-section, should be carefully investigated and analyzed by a competent soils engineer to determine potential impacts for development

If soil constraints are relatively localized, the extra cost to develop may cause a site to be uncompetitive in the marketplace. Buyers may not understand, or perceive, the required mitigation and the associated cost. If not properly mitigated, problems may occur during construction or after the community is complete. Such problems could cause financial harm and will damage a builder's reputation. The builder should understand the soil engineer's report, to determine whether constraints exist, and the cost to mitigate such constraints if they are present, before purchasing the land. If constraints are found, the purchase price can be negotiated based on the increased cost of building.

For many counties, the local Soil Conservation Service (SCS) reports and the National Geologic Survey provide general information regarding soil conditions and potential limitations. This information can be used to perform a cursory evaluation of soils on site and in the vicinity. In the absence of this information, it is critical that soil borings be completed on site and a reputable soils engineer provide information regarding the suitability of soils for the

Figure 3.6 Various layers of soil create a soil profile.

proposed uses. The report should discuss the characteristics of the soil and methods to mitigate potential problems.

Geology

Underlying geology can have significant financial impacts on development. In areas with poor soils, installing *caissons* to bedrock may be necessary. Greater depths to bedrock add cost. When bedrock is too shallow, it may be necessary to blast rock to install water and sewer lines. This, too, is expensive. Depth to bedrock has the potential to affect the layout and design of all built elements.

Depth to bedrock can also have a positive impact on development. Natural rock ledges can become natural retaining walls with verti-cal, or near vertical, slopes. This can save money through reduced need for concrete or stone retaining walls and creates a more natural appearance. Soil borings located across the site will identify depth to bedrock and can be used to develop a strategy for mitigation. Again, the SCS and the National Geologic Survey are useful sources of information.

Slope

Slope influences everything from road placement and access to the appropriate design of buildings. Slopes become even more important in northern climates because of snow and ice, and in areas of poor soils. Mapping slopes that relate to acceptable street grades and building designs helps the community designer minimize negative impacts. Slopes also provide an opportunity to separate clusters of housing, enhancing privacy and views, which can result in significant lot premiums.

In northern climates, many municipalities limit maximum street grades to 6 percent for collector streets and 8 percent for local streets, with greater restrictions for north-facing slopes. Maximum road grades at a stop sign can be as little as 4 percent. These standards are designed to allow vehicles safe stopping distances at typical design speeds. They also ensure that drivers can control the vehicles at all times. As roads are planned for steeper slopes, they must begin to run parallel to the slope to meet street grade standards.

Housing type is also influenced by slope. On smaller, narrow lots, the distance between buildings determines how much grade can be taken up in slope banks or by more expensive walls or extended foundations. Smaller front and back yards, and the need to drain water around buildings, also limit the amount of slope small lots can accommodate. In areas where basements are popular, a walkout lower level can be built to accommodate grade changes and minimize cut and fill. Minimizing cut and fill reduces site development expenses through lower earth-moving costs and reduced site disturbance that otherwise would require revegetation or stabilization.

The height of the lower level and the depth of the house determine what slope is appropriate for walkout homes. For example, a house that is 60 feet deep, sits on a 100-foot-deep lot, is 2 feet above the street, and has a 9-foot difference in elevation from the first floor to the lower level requires an 8.2 percent slope across the lot to provide a walkout and minimize cut and fill. The same house on a 60-foot-wide lot with 10-foot side yard setbacks will work on a maximum 3.8 percent street grade without the need for walls between units (see Figure 3.7). Larger building footprints, such as apartments and commercial buildings, are more difficult to place on sloping sites and can require significant grading or retaining walls.

In northern climates, on true north-facing slopes, road grades should be limited to 6 percent. When roads angle across the slope or are parallel to the slope, steep cut-and-fill slopes or retaining walls are necessary. Retaining walls on the southern side of the road will cast shadows over the road, increasing the chance for ice and snow build-up. With steep cut-and-fill slopes on roads, considering how driveways to lots will be created is also important. For example, wider uphill lots may be necessary to give a drive more length for getting up the slope, and access should generally be from the uphill side of the lot. Driveways with more

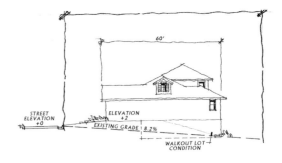

Credit: Courtesy of DTJ Design.

Figure 3.7 Sections illustrating the impact of slopes on housing.

than 15 percent grade are difficult for vehicles to negotiate and can cause vehicles to scrape as they enter or exit the drive and garage.

The following typical slope categories will help the community designer determine the best location for roadways, drives, and buildings:

- **0 percent to 4 percent.** No limitations for development
- **More than 4 percent to 6 percent.** Suitable for streets in any direction and mid-sized lots running parallel to the street; maximum grade for buildings with large, flat footprints, such as apartments and commercial buildings
- **More than 6 percent to 8 percent.** Suitable for local streets in any direction and walkout units on mid-sized to large lots

- **More than 8 percent to 12 percent.** Suitable for shallow unit walkouts, driveways, and local streets running generally perpendicular to the slope
- **More than 12 percent to 15 percent.** Suitable for development with special design features, including site walls, extended foundations, custom architecture, and walkout lower levels
- **More than 15 percent.** Generally unsuitable for development without significant increased cost and special design features

Hydrology

The system of surface and sub-surface water is referred to as *hydrology*. Water is a fragile resource and must be protected and weaved into the community design. Streams, wetlands, lakes, and rivers are valuable community amenities, and they are vital to our nation's environmental and economic health. Without clean water, we cannot grow the food or ingest the liquids necessary to sustain us. Without clean water, we cannot manufacture many of the products we take for granted in our daily lives.

All development, from farming to home building, disrupts the natural hydrological system. This disruption may take the form of increased chemical loads on waterways and ground water from fertilizers sprayed on agricultural lands, or increased *siltation* as a result of grading for a new road or building. The disruption may be the depletion of ground water through wells for crop irrigation or to serve population growth. It can even take the form of acid rain as airborne pollutants are washed to the ground in a storm. Each of these events has an immediate, and potentially lasting, impact on the environment.

Quality community design employs methods to minimize impacts to the site's hydrology and to mitigate those impacts that cannot be avoided. Vegetated buffer areas should be established adjacent to surface water, and runoff should be cleaned through bioswales, water gardens, and water-quality ponds. Water-quality ponds trap silt and heavy metals in runoff from roads before the water enters a natural drainageway. Bioswales capture even more pollutants from the water as plants slow water down and absorb nutrients. Nutrients in the runoff can cause algae growth, which reduces absorbed oxygen in the water and causes spikes in water temperature. Without this oxygen, fish and other aquatic creatures may die, and the rise in temperature may kill plants and animals. Water gardens (isolated depressions in the ground planted with water-tolerant plant material) take relatively clean water from rooftops and natural areas to support plants that thrive in wet conditions. These Smart Growth techniques are more sustainable, reduce environmental damage, and can cost less to implement.

At the Village of Autumn Lake (Figure 3.8), each of these methods was used to enhance the quality of runoff before it enters the lake. The lake serves as a regional detention facility and as a community amenity. Existing wetlands on site were also used to clean water. The wetland areas act as a portal to ground water. Storm water is cleaned with water-quality ponds and diverted to the wetlands. This process helps maintain ground-water levels and stream levels in the adjacent Stark-

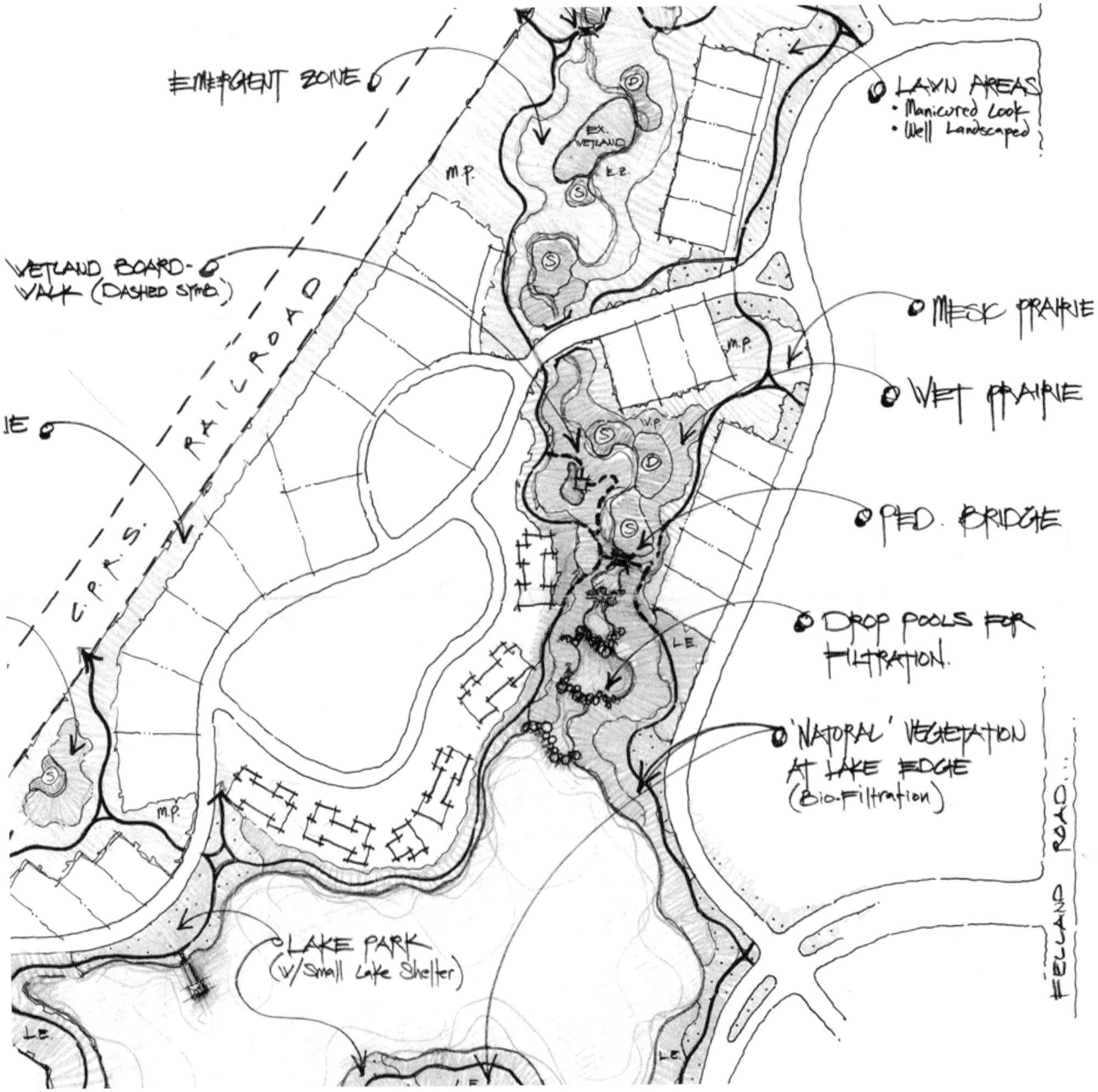
EMERGENT ZONE
LAWN AREAS
• Manicured Look
• Well Landscaped
WETLAND BOARD-WALK (DASHED SYMB.)
MESIC PRAIRIE
WET PRAIRIE
PED. BRIDGE
DROP POOLS FOR FILTRATION.
'NATURAL' VEGETATION AT LAKE EDGE (Bio-Filtration)
LAKE PARK (W/Small Lake Shelter)
C.P.R.S. RAILROAD
FELLAND ROAD
EX. WETLAND

Credit: Courtesy of DTJ Design.

Figure 3.8 Several innovative methods have been used at the Village of Autumn Lake to clean runoff before it enters the lake.

weather Creek basin. Water gardens on the island in the lake filter the water before it runs off into the lake.

Many wetlands are an important part of our natural resource. They filter runoff before it enters rivers and lakes, they provide habitat for a variety of birds and mammals, and they can be a ground-water recharge source. There are, however, differences in the function and quality of wetlands. High-quality wetlands perform the functions above and clean large amounts of water. They are usually hydrologically connected to larger water bodies that benefit from their cleaning function. Wetlands are regulated at both the federal and state levels to protect this resource,. The community designer should incorporate high-quality wetlands into the design of the community.

Low-quality wetlands perform the functions described above in a limited fashion. They might be isolated from other water bodies or the ground water. They might have little or no vegetation, resulting in minimal wildlife habitat. They might be small or have an intermittent water source. Some are man-made—for example, the result of a road fill or farm pond—and disappear when the man-made influence is removed. Unfortunately, in some jurisdictions, regulations do not distinguish between high-quality and low-quality wetlands. The two categories may have biological differences, but they are regulated in the same manner, which can make mitigation unnecessarily costly.

Wetland mitigation should be considered as a method to allow removal of low-quality wetlands by replacing them with high-quality wetlands. Some states have authorized the creation of *wetland mitigation banks*, whereby a developer might pay the bank for the right to fill a low-quality wetland. The mitigation bank uses the revenue to create a larger, functionally superior wetland to offset the loss of the lower-quality wetland. Typically, wetlands must be replaced at a greater ratio than 1:1, and it is preferred that the wetlands be replaced within the same regional watershed. Low-quality wetlands can also interfere with the reasonable and efficient use of land. Inefficient use of the land resource also has environmental implications: It can result in the need for additional paving, which has a higher embodied energy cost, it increases miles driven, and it increases runoff.

Climate

Site-specific climate, or *micro-climate*, has as much influence on community design as more regional climate considerations. Climate, and its related weather patterns, influence building design, road and driveway placement and grades, door and window placement, outdoor living spaces, even plant types and locations. Precipitation, in the form of rain or snow, wind, and *solar gain*, are the three most important climatic influences to consider in community design.

In northern climates, the effective road width and parking area are reduced by large accumulations of snow. Snow storage areas should be designed along streets and in parking lots. Larger detention areas, and even treed lawns, can function as snow storage areas. Small open areas can also be left at the end of streets or common drives so plows can push snow to a specific spot and move on. Roads oriented north and south will usually clear faster than roads oriented east and west because the low winter sun has a better opportunity to reach the ground, speeding melting. North-facing front doors and driveways will remain icy and snow covered longer than if they faced south, east, or west. As with each of the environmental considerations, there are no hard and fast rules; the community designer must strive to create a balance between competing elements.

Strong winds can literally move tons of snow onto buildings and pavement, causing hazards and increased removal costs. Specific design solutions can be implemented to minimize the negative effects of climatic influences. Strategic plantings create a windbreak and can be used to deposit snow in safe areas. Modifications to roof pitches, architectural details, or plantings can change the flow of wind over buildings, allowing the snow to fall to the ground instead of on the roof. Large open areas should be broken up by plantings to reduce wind speed and keep the snow on the ground. Evergreen trees and shrubs can buffer northern exposures from cold, creating an insulating space between the home and the winter winds.

Solar orientation can help heat the house in winter and cool the house in summer. Outdoor living areas that face the east will benefit from the warmth of the early morning sun, and the building can shield them from the hotter afternoon sun. Indoor living areas, protected by a canopy of deciduous leaves or large eaves, should face south to maximize winter solar gain and filtered summer light. In small-lot development, consideration must be given to the shadow patterns that homes create on adjacent properties. Maximizing the light in small courtyard spaces is important.

In hotter climates, the focus must shift to minimizing heat gain on indoor and outdoor living spaces, and controlling airflow to effect cooling breezes. Situating outdoor spaces to take advantage of afternoon shade, and creating deep eaves and overhangs are two methods to minimize heat gain. Incorporating water in key locations within the community can provide a tangible cooling effect, and the visual perception of the water can have a psychological cooling effect.

Vegetation and Tree Preservation

Existing vegetation has the potential to create significant value for any community. High on the list of community preferences is open space (AmericanLIVES, 1999), and open space is often defined as natural landscaped areas. In addition to being a visual amenity, existing vegetation can provide privacy, screening of unwanted views, cooling, and wind breaks, and it can give the community an image of being established for some time. Vegetation has a major role in establishing site character. Each of these influences has value in the buyer's mind. Value is diminished when sites are cleared of all trees (Figure 3.9).

Tree rows can become edges to land uses; they might be incorporated into a major boulevard; they can become focal points in an improved open space; they might define an open space trail; or they can separate groups of buildings. Shrub massing can give definition to an open space or hide drives and parking. Natural ground covers on steep slopes can reduce the erosion potential and minimize the need for mitigation. Specimen trees can be a unique

Figure 3.9 Clear-cutting is costly and reduces a site's inherent value.

feature on more expensive lots, resulting in lot premiums.

In areas with abundant trees, selective clearing may be necessary to provide views from homes and allow light to reach the ground. Additional clearing may be required in fire-prone areas. A brush-free zone around the house, combined with using fire-resistant building materials and trimming tree branches above the ground, can minimize the loss due to wildfire.

Before making any decisions about existing vegetation, it is necessary to first complete an assessment of the type and quality of the plant material. An experienced arborist or landscape architect should inventory each tree in good health and more than 2 inches in *diameter at breast height (dbh)*. The inventory should include the size, species, and condition of the tree. A determination should be made regarding the potential for the tree to be successfully relocated if the community design dictates that. Shrub massing should also be located and identified on a map. In areas of heavy woods, it may be necessary to inventory only larger trees (4 inches dbh or greater), but it is more important to consider the potential for windfall along a newly opened edge here. Trees that have grown protected from wind are more susceptible to wind damage.

Generally, it is important to not disturb the land within the *crown*, or outside diameter, of the tree. Most shallow-rooted tree species are stressed or can die from only a foot of soil placed within this area. Even construction traffic over the root zone can kill a tree over time. Construction fencing delimiting a "no disturbance" zone should be erected around those trees that will be saved, with contractor fines enforced for violations. Steeper grades, tree wells, and retaining walls can be used to minimize disturbance and preserve existing vegetation. Special design considerations are required to ensure survival of the tree and conformance to the character and image of the community.

Habitat

A diverse wildlife population generally indicates that the ecosystem is healthy and should be protected, or enhanced. It is important to consider the impact of change due to development on both a regional and site scale. On a regional scale, wildlife corridors and woodlots should be identified and analyzed as to the wildlife present and the quality of the habitat. If areas of the site contribute to the regional habitat, wildlife corridors should be left intact if feasible. These corridors can be continuous woodlands, streams, or rivers, or even hedgerows. They allow larger wildlife to move undisturbed from feeding areas to bedding areas. Isolated woodlots provide shelter and food for a variety of animals and birds, and these areas should also be preserved if possible.

In addition to preservation, enhancing the quality of habitat is possible through selective planting and design. The objective is to provide opportunity for a stable food source and protection. Small lakes and ponds planted with a variety of plant species create habitats that encourage diversity of animal species. Connected open spaces and trails at least 100 feet wide allow animals to move more freely throughout the community. This dimension can be reduced in areas with more vegetated cover. Strategically placed culverts, or "critter crossings," can provide a safe path for wildlife to cross busy roads.

The federal government, and many states, have laws that protect threatened or endangered species. On the one hand, some people believe the loss of any animal or plant species is a tragedy, and on the other, some people believe that species have emerged and disappeared since the beginning of time and the process is, in part, the natural course of affairs. The debate still rages about the science that creates a direct link from certain development activities to the loss of any specific species, and about the value to the ecosystem of any one species. Of concern to many environmentalists is that the loss or endangerment of plants and animals indicates damage to the ecosystem, the impact of which may not be fully known. One potential solution is that, when the public believes there is sufficient benefit to protecting threatened or endangered species, the public should invest in the protection of its habitat through purchasing that land at fair market value and not place the burden of protecting the public's interest on the backs of the building industry. A state's Division of Natural Resources may have preliminary mapping that indicates the possible presence of endangered species. If species or habitat is identified, it is prudent to work with an experienced biologist or botanist to determine the best method to preserve habitat or mitigate habitat destruction.

Environmental considerations are important to the success of any community design, particularly those in undeveloped areas. This sensitivity will make the community more desirable, enhance property values, speed sales, and reduce opposition. The community character evolves from the inherent qualities of the site. Ideally, the community should integrate into the existing environment. Design solutions should evolve from a detailed understanding of environmental considerations.

Viewsheds

People appreciate the site through views into, throughout, and from the site. Understanding and controlling views can expose the beauty and hide the warts of the site. To document the views, walking the entire site searching for good and bad views is necessary. Driving the adjacent streets to inventory views of the site from adjacent properties is also necessary. Views to the site can provide marketing "windows" that display site assets and can have an impact on neighbors' perceptions of the site. This may become an important consideration in mitigating opposition to new development. Views to special features on the site should also be documented. The view analysis should discuss whether the views are *foreground* (views close to the viewer), *middle ground* (views slightly farther away), or *background* views (distant views). Each view is affected to a greater, or lesser, extent by what happens in the foreground.

Views can result in lot or unit premiums for good views, or they can require significant screening or buffering to hide bad views. Community design strategies should maximize the positive impact of good views and, conversely,

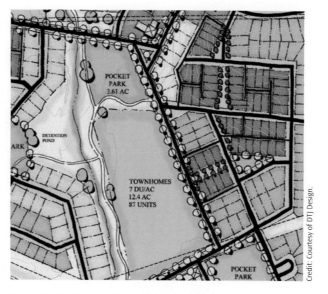

Figure 3.10 **The site plan for Meadow Sweet Farm preserved the best views from major streets.**

minimize the negative impact of poor views. The community designer must evaluate the impact of views from the perspective of the entire community and not relinquish views to only a few select lots. At Meadow Sweet Farm in Erie, Colorado, a long-range, or background, view to Longs Peak, part of the continental divide, was celebrated by a straight street focused directly at the highest point of the peak. This placement reinforces the image of the Colorado lifestyle each time a person drives northwest along the street, and it provides a great view for the entire community instead of a select few (Figure 3.10). Similarly, roads terminate with views to parks, open spaces, or lakes to highlight the amenities designed for the community.

Public acceptance of the community is, in large part, controlled by what people see when they pass by. Thought must be given to what

Figure 3.11 Homes facing the street create an inviting edge.

the views are from adjacent properties and streets. A softer edge along the street may have a favorable impression, while a rear yard lined with a tall privacy fence may be a negative. At McKay Landing in Broomfield, Colorado, the homes face the adjacent arterial instead of backing to it, as in most cities (Figures 3.11 and 3.12). Traffic impacts are mitigated by creating a landscaped boulevard and setting the homes above the street. The homes are alley accessed, and the front porches look across the road to an adjacent lake

Sharing views to amenities or open spaces can reap benefits when negotiating approvals with the neighboring properties. Know what part of the site is visible from adjacent land and discuss that as part of the view analysis. Respect the neighbors by enhancing, or at least maintaining, their view if possible.

Noise
Noise from highways, major streets, trains, airplanes, and adjacent land uses can have an impact on the appeal of the neighborhood. Common mitigation techniques (high walls or fences) create visual barriers and do not completely eliminate the sound. In some areas of intense noise—for example, near take-off and

approach zones for airports—building mitigation techniques must be used. Additional insulation, double-paned windows, and air-conditioning are required in areas in which the average daily noise level is above 65 decibels. These noise contours are mapped and available from the Federal Aviation Administration.

Although home buyers may become acclimated to noise over time, marketing homes in areas of high noise levels is difficult. Special discounts may be necessary where the noise levels are the worst, resulting in lower overall revenues. An alternative would be to plan open space uses instead of housing in affected areas. Tall *berming* and landscaping should be used to deflect the noise above the adjacent homes.

Visual screening can also be used to hide the noise source.

Man-Made Influences

In contrast to environmental influences, man-made influences can be modified somewhat to support the community design or enhance various features. Off-site improvements can be made that change the very nature of how the community is perceived, or even constructed. The community builder can influence how these improvements are completed and financed. For example, a new road could be built that provides access to a site away from a potentially negative land use. This road may change the sequence of arrival, having a posi-

Figure 3.12 Fence canyons can make the community appear less friendly.

tive impact on the community's land use and value. The community builder may facilitate the process by lobbying the jurisdiction responsible for building the road, or the builder could help fund the construction.

An analysis of man-made influences then must address what influences are present on or around a given site; how much flexibility there is to modify those influences, and at what price; and what the value is of the resulting benefits. In addition, the analysis must also address what the capacity of the entire system is for each man-made influence. If there is not sufficient capacity in any part of the system, determining the cost and feasibility to improve the capacity may be necessary. *Moratoria* are one method municipalities use to halt new development until system capacity is increased. Being proactive and providing potential solutions can mean the difference between having or not having a new community.

Roads and Access

For the purposes of this book, roads can be considered a way to get to the site, while access is the way to enter the site. Each has a slightly different impact on the quality of the community. Roads to the site begin to establish community character by the sequence of arrival. How people will come to the site, what the visual quality is of what they see on their way, and what changes might take place over time must be carefully considered. Marketing of the community is influenced by the quality of the arrival and the journey home. The local capital-improvements plan should be analyzed to determine long-range improvements and their impact.

Thought needs to be given to road capacity and the potential cost to improve. Alternate forms of arrival should also be considered. Providing light rail, or other mass transit, could reduce the obligation to improve adjacent roadways. Multiple points of site access may also reduce the need for adjacent roadway improvements. Major road improvements not only are costly, but they also can have significant negative impacts on community character and make obtaining public acceptance of the community more difficult. Neighbors often fight new community development on the basis of increased traffic and congestion. Strategies to minimize traffic congestion must be considered.

Access to the site is complicated by basic engineering and safety considerations. Road grades must allow for safe stopping distances, and location must provide sufficient sight distances. On busier streets, there must be enough room for acceleration and deceleration lanes, and for stacking of vehicles at intersections. In more urban areas, accommodating traffic-signal spacing is necessary. There should be enough space at the entry to develop a sense of arrival. It is important to provide access that supports the desired community character and extends this sense of arrival beyond the entry.

Locating the entry and access adjacent to an existing site feature or amenity is one method to extend the marketing impact beyond the entry. Other means include sensitive alignment around natural features, sensitive site grading, and quality enhancement of the street by creating boulevards and small, unique spaces along the roadway. The community character might include open-space elements, and the natural amenity supports that perception. Repeatedly touching the access road to the site amenity reinforces the amenity as a key site feature and helps to visually balance the community. The design for Siena, a large master-planned community in Broomfield, Colorado, places a major road along the entire length of a natural open space and trail (Figure 3.13), which effectively establishes the community as one that values these amenities. This is a positive contrast to other large subdivisions that simply put a fence along the street.

The design of the street cross-section has a tremendous impact on the desirability of the community. Narrow, tree-lined streets with branches arching over the roadway evoke an image of calm and safety. Vehicles move slowly down the street, and the driver's focus is on the quality of the homes and yards. The primary purpose of local residential streets is to provide access to adjacent homes. The need for moving large numbers of cars quickly must become secondary to the quality of life on the street. Wide streets with fast-moving cars are less inviting to pedestrians and create safety hazards. The primary purpose of these larger streets is to move a greater number of cars quickly. Balancing the need to move vehicles through the community with the desires of the residents for quiet, safe streets is important. "Chapter Five: Community Design" discusses in more detail the importance of appropriate street design.

One method to decrease the concentration of vehicles on any one street is to increase the number of connections to adjacent roadways. This strategy causes traffic to disperse more evenly, resulting in fewer vehicles on each road, which in turn allows for a narrower street cross-section. Traffic-calming devices, including *traffic circles, landscape bump-outs* at intersections, and *speed humps,* also slow traffic and create a safer street. Recent studies have shown that narrower streets with slow speeds actually have lower accident rates than higher-speed streets; and, when accidents occur, the magnitude of injury and property damage is much lower (Residential Street Typology and Injury Accident Frequency, Swift and Associates, 1997).

Water and Sewer

On a regional scale, the availability of water and sewer service can determine the site's suitability for development and can dictate the type of community that can be designed. Without municipal water and sewer service, most development is restricted to a low-density community with homes on individual well and septic systems. For larger properties, a community well and water-treatment system, and a package sewer treatment plant may be viable alternatives.

Extending regional water and sewer systems to the site can be very costly and difficult to justify without additional financing sources. Some states allow the creation of special districts or metropolitan districts that have the authority to issue bonds to pay for major infrastructure investment. The bonds are repaid by revenue generated by taxes on improved property within the district. These are usually private-issue bonds that are not backed by the municipality and carry a higher interest rate. A lower-cost, municipal-backed bond is similar to a special district and is referred to as a *TIF,* or *Tax Increment Financed* bond. These bonds are repaid by the difference in the tax revenue (the increment) from the

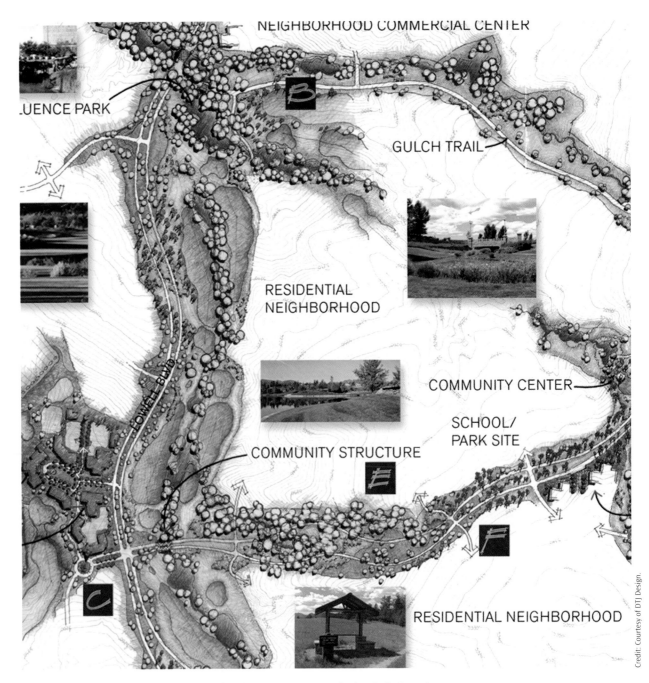

NEIGHBORHOOD COMMERCIAL CENTER

...LUENCE PARK

GULCH TRAIL

RESIDENTIAL
NEIGHBORHOOD

COMMUNITY CENTER

SCHOOL/
PARK SITE

COMMUNITY STRUCTURE

RESIDENTIAL NEIGHBORHOOD

LOWELL BLVD

Figure 3.13 Significant open space along a major street creates a relaxing feel along the street.

undeveloped property to the improved property. Because both approaches require adding taxes to property, they require public approval. "Chapter Seven: Financing Community" outlines how the community builder/developer should allocate financial resources to create the necessary infrastructure and amenities.

On-site water and sewer systems have increased design flexibility. These systems can respond to various layouts without significant differences in cost. Engineering rules, however, can affect how these systems influence the visual quality of the community. For example, when sewer lines are allowed to run through open space, the required manholes can be blended into landscaped areas and generally hidden. Unfortunately, some municipalities require maintenance or access roads, which defeat the visual benefit of putting the infrastructure in open space. When sewer lines are required to run in the street (for easier maintenance), the manhole covers can become an obstacle in the roadway. This problem is made more acute on curved roadways, where additional manholes are required. The best solution is to allow a combination of approaches, depending on the design of the street and the function of the open space. Similarly, water lines run either in the street or off to one side. When they run off to one side, trees may be restricted from being planted within several feet of either side of the line.

Gas, Electric, Telephone, and Cable

Together, these utilities are often referred to as *dry utilities*. Their layout and design is influenced more by cost and efficiency than by site limitations. The utility companies determine what works best for their system operation,

maintenance, and design for those criteria. Each utility has either *pedestals* for connections or access, or signs that indicate the presence of buried pipe or cable. The pedestals are on concrete pads and typically require unobstructed area around the front and sides of the pedestal cabinet.

The impact on community design is usually visual. To minimize the negative visual impact of these pedestals, the community designer must work with the utility companies from the beginning to influence where pedestals are constructed. This is true also for multifamily buildings on which service meters are often ganged on exposed walls. The building design must address the location of meters and provide visual screening.

Storm Water

Careful consideration must be given to how storm water will be handled within the community. One approach is to capture the storm water in pipes as quickly as possible and move it to a *detention basin*. This approach involves curbs and gutters, catch basins, *storm inlets*, manholes, *drop structures*, culverts, *headwalls*, and lots of pipe. It concentrates runoff, making downstream improvements more costly. Where large volumes of water are collected along roadways, this approach may be necessary to ensure that water does not build up on the road or impede traffic and safety. In addition, in areas of steep slope, collecting the water quickly to minimize the potential for erosion may be necessary.

Another approach is to slow the concentration of water and divert it through a system of natural swales, small ponds and check dams, ponds, water gardens, and constructed

Figure 3.14 Drainage ways can be designed to become community amenities.

wetlands. This method requires more land area for swales and ponds, and results in a more rural appearance. With the concentration of runoff slowed, some water percolates into the ground, recharging ground water and reducing detention requirements. In semi-arid environments, water in this system can reduce the required irrigation needs for trees and shrubs.

Some combination of these two approaches is often the most cost-effective and aesthetically pleasing solution to storm-water control. Natural systems should be used where practical and feasible, with pipes and inlets used where necessary. The natural system should be incorporated into the community amenity program and celebrated as a feature. In River Run in Boise, Idaho (Figure 3.14),

small rivulets and wetlands create a valuable amenity at the rear of each home. This combination provides a sense of enclosure to the rear yards, enhances privacy, and creates visual diversity in the community.

Land Use

The side effects of adjacent land uses can have either a strong positive or negative influence on building community. It is easy to understand that a golf course would raise property values for an adjacent site, while a landfill would significantly diminish values. The community design would embrace the first relationship and seek to mitigate the second. Less obvious is how to address similar land uses that might have either positive or negative influences. The community designer must evaluate each condition and determine whether it is a positive, negative, or neutral influence on the community.

One method to help make this determination is to think about how the community might be connected to, and visually blended with, the adjacent land use. If the connections are awkward, or it is difficult to form a visually cohesive neighborhood, the adjacent land use could be considered a negative, and the community design might include screening or buffering. The straight, hard, visual edge of the community in Figure 3.15 requires a softer response by the neighboring community, to minimize the harsh line between the two neighborhoods. The park on the edge (Fig-

ure 3.16), however, creates a good opportunity to link the parks and have a seamless connection between neighborhoods.

Land-use compatibility is more a function of scale and detail than actual use. Given proper scale, detailing of buildings, texture of the community, and a variety of commercial and residential uses can exist side by side in a manner that supports each use. Countless examples of small, pedestrian-scaled commercial centers that create a heart within a residential community exist across the United States. To be successful, the focus must remain on pedestrian connectivity, encouraging walking to the commercial uses and activity (outdoor plazas, sidewalk cafes, farmer's market) on the street. Large-scale buildings (multistory office

Figure 3.15 A hard edge, with no visual relief, should be softened with a looser development pattern.

Figure 3.16 Parks and open spaces can cross neighborhood boundaries to effectively link different developments together.

buildings or big-box retail) and parking lots overpower the neighborhood, and the community designer must provide screening and/or transitional uses.

Historical and Archeological Factors

Culturally significant historical or archeological sites within the community can become the catalyst for a project theme or character that reflects the spirit of the place. Incorporating these features into the community design shows a respect for the past and a commitment to the larger community. A review of historical documents and photographs for the area can suggest whether more in-depth study should be completed. Even if the site does not have historical or archeological significance, this review can help the community designer formulate ideas for a believable community

vision. The intent is not to replicate the past but to create a connection in the residents' minds between the history of the region and the place in which they live.

At the Windler Homestead mixed-use community, the historically significant homestead not only became a feature of the plan but also suggested an overall theme. The homestead (Figure 3.17) anchors a linear park connecting the residential neighborhood to the "Old Town" commercial area at the interchange. This transition from a rural farm area, through a residential area, into the town center is a microcosm of a small town (Figure 3.18). The residential area supports the overall vision through small, tree-lined streets, detached sidewalks, and alley-loaded homes. Within the "Old Town," two- and three-story commercial buildings surround a small town square, extending the open space into the center of the community (Figure 3.19). Along the highway, an historical marker details the significance of the Windler Homestead. To complete the link to the past, the sales center displays artifacts from the homestead and describes pioneer life in the area (Figure 3.20).

Evaluating historical or archeological resources can delay construction of the community; however, the cultural value of the resource can offset this expense. Some state or local historical societies will underwrite a portion of the cost of the investigation and can help preserve artifacts for later display. Because many of these sites are best left in public trust, it is wise to propose that the historical or archeological site be dedicated to the public and credit be given to reduce the amount of public land dedication required for the entire community.

Community Values and Perceptions

Because most projects are approved with input from the community, understanding how adjacent neighborhoods and the larger community will evaluate and voice their opinions about a design proposal is important. An analysis of past project approvals and the interaction with different neighborhood groups will shed some light on the attitudes of the community. Speaking with the community development director or planning director can save countless hours pursuing a community plan that has little or no chance of approval. Even the best community design is worthless if the designers can't obtain approvals.

Figure 3.17 The original Windler Homestead became the driving force behind the creation of the "Old Town" theme.

Figure 3.18 The site plan evolved around the homestead to create a small town.

Figure 3.19 A town square anchors the smaller retail and office uses of the "Old Town" section of the Windler Homestead community.

Figure 3.20 A community center/sales center is designed to complement the existing homestead buildings.

Armed with the knowledge about the community attitudes and perceptions, the community designers can better understand what battles they face and can begin to develop a strategy to counteract opposition. These strategies are discussed in more detail in "Chapter 6: Regulatory Issues."

Low-Impact Development

One goal of the community builder should be to minimize disturbance of the environment as much as practical. Several interrelated strategies help achieve this goal. They include minimal grading, enhanced storm-water infiltration, utilization of *bio-retention*, replanting with native species, replicating the existing hydrology, and preserving and using natural areas as site amenities. Together, these strategies can have a significant positive effect on the health of the environment and the quality of the community.

Avoiding areas of steep slopes, narrower street widths, specialized architecture, and natural retaining walls helps minimize grading. Tree wells preserve natural vegetation and can allow for steeper slopes returning to natural grade. A 2:1 grade instead of a 3:1 grade on a 10-foot fill reduces the width of the disturbance by more than 10 horizontal feet. At Rehberg Ranch in Billings, Montana, tree wells (Figure 3.21) and small retaining walls reduced the disturbance at just one drainage crossing by more than 30 feet horizontally. This allowed the natural drainage to remain as the primary image for the community.

Minimizing the concentration of storm-water runoff, fanning swales to sheet drain water across porous soils, utilizing permeable pavement, creating multiple drainage channels, and using *bio-filtration* to clean storm water all increase the amount of water that may percolate back into the soil. This minimizes siltation of existing water bodies and recharges the ground water. Less silt in the water minimizes heat gain, resulting in less algae growth and more dissolved oxygen in the water available for aquatic wildlife. Biologists and botanists design bioswales to remove heavy metals, phosphorus, nitrogen, and other pollutants from the run-off stream. These treatment trains effectively clean water as it moves through the community.

Figure 3.21 Tree wells can be used to save existing trees.

Figure 3.22 Native plantings were used to give the Tallyn's Reach entry the image of an old foundation wall emerging from the landscape.

The most effective strategy for rapid revegetation is to replant disturbed areas with native vegetation. These plants are most accustomed to the soils and availability of water, and are better able to survive the stress of planting. Replanting should replicate the natural plant groupings and location of the native species. Central to this concept is the idea of preserving existing vegetation where possible. These natural areas, enhanced with additional native plantings, can become community amenities (Figure 3.22). Properly designed, native plantings help achieve an image that is consistent with the spirit of the place

Opportunities and Constraints of Site Context

The preceding inventory and analysis should now be summarized in written and graphic form. This summary should present only information that has an effect on the design of the community. The information presented should make a connection between what is important from the site analysis and how the community design might reflect that importance. This connection supports the design decisions and helps the public and regulatory agencies understand why the community plan makes sense. Unnecessary information clutters the summary and confuses the audience.

Summarizing the opportunities and constraints of the site is particularly important in communicating the unique design opportunities inherent in each site. This is even more important in large master-planned communities dominated by production builders. Their attention to the efficiency of home production requires an even stronger reliance on the qualities of the site to differentiate neighborhoods

*Creative community design
is not constrained by the site
boundary nor the drawing
board.*

and communities. More effort must be given to creative community design to offset the prejudices that many communities have against standardized home design. As national builders become even larger and their focus on national branding stronger, this issue will become more critical to obtaining community approvals.

Elements that are opportunities should be supported by a discussion of how they might be weaved into the community design. Major features might become the skeleton of the community design. Constraints should be supported by a discussion of the steps necessary to mitigate the potential problems. A strategy should be presented that turns development constraints into site opportunities. For example, the poor soils at Autumn Lake became the driving force behind the creation of a lake, which is the centerpiece of the community story and vision.

A good opportunities-and-constraints summary will prioritize the various elements deemed important for the design of the community. Certain environmental influences cannot be modified and begin to take precedence. Other environmental influences can be modified somewhat to facilitate the community design. Man-made elements usually have more flexibility, yet it is important to know at what price. The opportunities-and-constraints summary should evaluate the risk and reward of modifying any element.

The creative community designer also looks beyond the confines of the site to determine opportunities and constraints. Two principles can guide this effort. The first is that creative community design is not constrained by the site boundary. The second is that creative community design is not constrained by the drawing board. The following examples are helpful in understanding these concepts.

Creative community design is not constrained by the site boundary. At McKay Landing, in Broomfield, Colorado, the relatively nondescript site sloped to the east and away from strong mountain views. The project consists of 887 units on approximately 220 acres. There are five main housing types, including sixplex townhomes with detached garages; a fourplex front- and rear-loaded townhome; alley-loaded, detached single-family homes; conventional front-loaded, single-family detached homes; three-car, move-up, single-family homes on larger lots; and larger, luxury, single-family detached homes. Small pocket parks provide open space within easy walking distance of each home.

McKay Lake plays an important role in defining the community, yet the lake is not even a part of the property. Located on public land to the east, McKay Lake is a reservoir for the neighboring city. The lake is approximately 73 acres in size and has a wonderful, soft edge. Trees, reeds, and native grasses come down to the lake edge. Wildlife abounds in the natural habitat. Recognizing this opportunity has been critical to the success of McKay Landing (Figure 3.23).

The community edge embraces the lake, with alley-loaded homes fronting on the north-south arterial (Zuni Street), and with a large, landscaped boulevard protecting the homes from the distractions of traffic. Visitor parking is in small bays running parallel to the street. This access lane creates an additional layer of landscape between the homes and the

Figure 3.23 The McKay Landing site plan builds from the site context.

Figure 3.24 An additional landscape buffer increases the desirability of living along a major street.

street (Figure 3.24). The homes sit above the road to ensure great views to the lake. A three-rail open fence defines the public and private spaces.

Main streets into and out of the community emanate from the lake and open-space corridor bordering the property, offering terrific views of McKay Lake. These view corridors link the lake with the large, central open space and establish a connection to the adjacent visual amenity. A crushed-stone trail (Figure 3.25) winds through the landscape of the main entry boulevard, extending the visual impact of the entry deep into the community. An additional seven acres was dedicated on the east side of Zuni Street to complement land already proposed for a regional park. This park reinforces the visual tie to the lake from the community.

The homes exhibit an architectural style dubbed Western Waterfront. The simple gables and dormers are similar to New England residential architecture, and the materials and bracket details give the buildings a decidedly western flair (Figures 3.26, 3.27, and 3.28). This architectural image was derived from the site's relationship to McKay Lake. The theme is extended to the entry, where a simple wooden sign hangs from a large timber. The battered stone column completes the connection to the mountains of the West.

The community center includes a community room, pool and change rooms, a deli, and even a day-care area. These uses will benefit the entire community and bring life to the community center year-round. The building is designed to give the impression of a cluster of small buildings (Figure 3.29), reminiscent of a

Figure 3.25 A crushed-stone trail is an inviting footpath.

Figure 3.26 The architecture of McKay Landing has a blend of New England waterfront and western features.

Figure 3.27 **Small details reinforce the architectural theme found throughout McKay Landing.**

small waterfront town. Large spaces are designed to facilitate community gatherings. Weddings, graduation parties, and home owners' meetings are anticipated events. A park, playground, and school complement the community center and will become the heart of the community.

The waterfront image is enhanced by the signage and neighborhood monuments. The name, McKay Landing, evokes an image of a waterfront. A graphic of ducks landing in the reeds are found on all community and neighborhood markers, and reinforce the community image. A large bronze sculpture of ducks landing anchors the outdoor gathering place at the community center. Each design element was in response to the presence of McKay Lake near, but not on, the site. Looking beyond the site boundary inspired the theme and charac-

Figure 3.28 **The architecture of the buildings wraps patio spaces, enclosing them as part of the overall building design.**

Figure 3.29 The McKay Landing community center has the appearance of a cluster of smaller buildings.

ter at McKay Landing. The community enjoyed approximately 30 sales a month combined in all five home types. The City of Broomfield holds McKay Landing up as an example of the type of community welcome in the city. Looking beyond the project boundary allowed the developer to achieve the public's goal of connecting new developments to the surrounding city fabric instead of allowing isolated neighborhoods.

Creative community design should not be constrained by the drawing board. Simply put, this means that some opportunities are not as much design driven as they are finance or approval driven. At a small country club in southern Wisconsin, the community builder was looking to expand his presence in the market by building several niche communities in

various cities. Land adjacent to the existing golf course was limited and would not produce enough units to create a viable project. Either the project would have to be abandoned, or a creative solution would have to be found.

A careful analysis of the site and the golf course revealed a significant amount of underutilized land adjacent to the clubhouse and hole 1. (See Figure 3.30). The clubhouse was a converted farmhouse and did not function well for a golf club. Parking and access were informal, and parking tended to spill over into the lawn. Additional discussions with members of the golf course highlighted a desire to upgrade the clubhouse. An opportunity arose to resolve the golf club's current problems and create additional developable land for a new community.

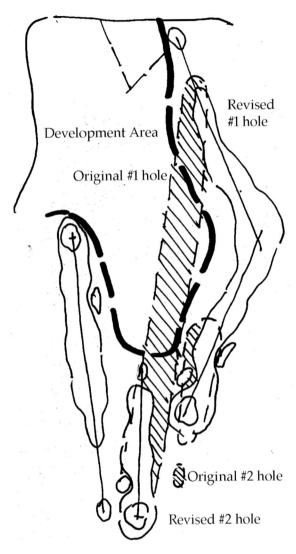

Development Area

Revised #1 hole

Original #1 hole

Original #2 hole

Revised #2 hole

Credit: Courtesy of The Design Alliance, Ltd.

Figure 3.30 The original plan for Lauderdale Lakes Country Club.

The club membership was fond of the course, and many members played several times per week. It was important to minimize disruption as much as possible and maintain the feel of the existing course. Several alternatives were presented to the club leadership, and a plan that moved only two holes was deemed worthy of additional study. The plan proposal that the #1 green would be left intact and become the #2 green. This created a dogleg right, making the hole more challenging. Hole 2 remained a short par three. The fairways were realigned to create a buildable, 9 plus-or-minus-acre parcel in the center of the golf course (Figure 3.31).

Key to the success of the plan was the building of a new clubhouse designed for golf. The plan moved the clubhouse south and east, and a new parking lot and access are visible north of the club building. A small grill and patio space overlook the ninth green. Each of the 48 townhomes has golf-course frontage and premiums, and each is designed for maintenance-free living. The homes stagger along the fairway to provide a nicer edge for the golfer and to create small, intimate spaces between buildings. A large, central landscaped area acts as a focal point at the front of each home.

As additional incentive, a portion of each homeowner's association dues was ear-marked for golf-course maintenance. This concept not only reduces the maintenance expense of the club but also ensures that the course will be well maintained and continue to add value to the adjacent community. To be successful, opportunities that are not constrained by the drawing board must be win-win for every

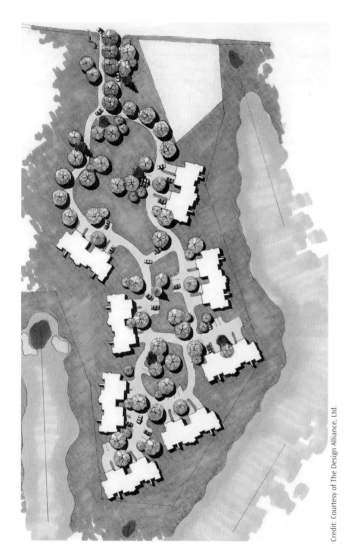

Credit: Courtesy of The Design Alliance, Ltd.

party involved. This requirement can be accomplished by looking at the needs of each party to determine whether any solutions meet more than one need. Ideally, any additional expenses can be offset through negotiation; however, some expenses might need to be justified by good will, speed of approvals, or visibility.

Opportunities and constraints guide the creation of the community vision and final design. Quality community design evolves from an in-depth understanding of these opportunities and constraints, and from creative problem-solving. The community builder must continually challenge the design team to seek the best solution for the community. What is best for the community design often translates into what is best for the community builder. When the community is completed with skill and experience, and the opportunities and constraints are incorporated into the community design, the understanding of site context creates significant value for the community builder.

Figure 3.31 The new site plan for Lauderdale Lakes created a townhome parcel surrounded by golf.

CHAPTER 4
Community Visioning

Planning for a Community Vision

Controlling the Vision

Community visioning is the process of bringing a community idea to life in the minds of the builder, the regulators, and ultimately, the buyers. The purpose is to translate a two-dimensional world of land plans to a three-dimensional representation through sketches, photographs, and models. Ideally, both the plans and the three-dimensional representations are developed concurrently, whereby each influences the other to make a better community. The intent is to help buyers, community leaders, and the development team understand what the community will look like and how it will live, before it is built. That understanding is enhanced by a focus on the details that express the character of the place. A community-vision document guides the design process to ensure that the community, as envisioned, becomes reality.

The value of a community vision is best realized when it is understood that community vision is as much a marketing concept as it is a design concept, developed together in an integrated approach. The community builder must help buyers visualize themselves living in the community. The investment in design and building is returned through easier approvals, faster absorption, higher prices, and enhanced reputation.

Buyers are attracted to a well-defined vision. People enjoy and remember well-designed places. The design may be a connection to history or represent buyers' values. The community stands out from standard subdivisions and suggests a more immediate "sense of place." In addition to attracting more people, a well-designed community means buyers are often willing to pay a premium for the opportunity to be part of something unique and the chance to feel connected to their neighbors. As they develop a passion for where they live, initial buyers become an active sales force, recruiting friends to live there also.

When the community builder has an initial vision for the community, a skilled team of designers who can simulate the three-dimension components can help articulate that vision. An appropriate vision should be based on the needs and desires of the buyer, the site history and context, and the expectations of the larger community. The site analysis and opportunities-and-constraints summary present clues to what this vision might be, and they can identify key site-based components of the vision. Without clear ideas emanating from the site, the community vision might reflect the history of the region or recognizable cultural influences. Where possible, the community vision should always take clues from the site's physical, cultural, or historical context.

Community visioning is, in essence, place-making. It is a balance between creating a memory and fulfilling an expectation the buyers may have. The vision is expressed through words and pictures and is utilized in presentations to city staff, planning commissions, and city councils; marketing materials also convey this vision. It is represented in the development pattern, mix of uses, and variety of densities. It is realized in the built environment through homes and community buildings, landscape and site furnishings, signage and entry monuments, walls, fencing, lighting, and other community elements. Community vision is an important element in the purchasing decision of today's more sophisticated buyers. They have been educated to be more aware of the nuances of what they buy, and they react favorably to quality design and materials. Many buyers also seek a sense of community

or belonging with their neighbors. Creating these connections through the community life is one goal of a community vision.

The following three examples illustrate different visions for three different parts of the country; each example represents a different market and historical context, and each has a different story to tell.

At Pabst Farms in Oconomowoc, Wisconsin, the historic farm buildings were a catalyst for the architectural character of the community vision, and the forms, textures, and colors were used to reinforce the connection to the history of the site. Located 40 miles west of Milwaukee, Pabst Farms was the dairy farm of the famous Pabst brewing family. The main farmhouse, barns, and other out buildings were built with a distinctive, flared red roof and concrete walls. The buildings are visible from surrounding streets and Interstate 94. The public associates these buildings with the farm, and many people are familiar with the history of the place. New buildings that exhibited a similar form and color would immediately be linked to Pabst Farms.

The vision for Pabst Farms relies on this visual connection to the site. Community identity along I-94 was designed to extend the image of the farm buildings to the edge of the community. A building reminiscent of a small well house was created, and a remnant foundation wall was extended to provide a place for the community name. (Figure 4.1) This is a powerful image that connects the site buildings to the community name and to the history of the place. Additional community signage exhibits elements of this character while not copying it directly. These features preserve the

Figure 4.1 The community signage for Pabst Farms reflects the history of the site.

overall community link to the past while creating a newer visual connection for the various residential neighborhoods.

The connection to the history of the community has been further enhanced by creating a vision for the community retail and office core that reflects the architecture of the older section of the adjacent town. (Figure 4.2) Founded in 1837 by immigrants, Oconomowoc was the regional center for a larger farming community and evolved into a playground for wealthy families from the greater Chicago area. The older buildings in downtown Oconomowoc are heavily influenced by northern European architecture. They were built by craftsman intent on leaving a legacy of good design and workmanship.

An updated interpretation of that architectural style reinforces the historic character of Pabst Farms and supports the vision of the community. The communities figurative "Main Street" is reserved for small boutique shops that have colorful window displays and sidewalk activity (Figure 4.3). *Big-box retailers* are welcome if they *skin* their stores with smaller, more intimate retail shops along the Main Street. They have been encouraged to allow multiple points of access into their stores. Many of the large discount retailers already have several semi-independent operations within the large box. These might include optical dispensing, banks, or food. One solution is to create a quasi-storefront for each of these uses and allow access into the larger store

Figure 4.2 The existing Town Hall.

must translate the building program needs and the buyers' expected community amenities into a vision that works with the site. Fortunately, in many instances, people are attracted to a site because of its innate character. A vision that exploits that character can have a positive effect on buyers.

For the community of Stillwater, along the Colorado River in western Colorado, buyers seek an active recreation lifestyle replete with golf, horseback riding, and fishing. A vision for a western ranch, on which guests are pampered in a rustic, yet elegant, setting, was created for the community. This vision especially appeals to the higher-end buyers that might live along the golf course; however, homeowners in all price ranges benefit from the image and character of the community. This vision touches the expectations that people have of a western ranch and creates lasting memory points. This will give Stillwater a distinct advantage in the marketplace, allowing it to successfully compete with other master-planned communities.

The "western ranch" vision was articulated through a combination of land use, architectural detailing, and landscape features. Designed as a country community comprising three villages, Stillwater exhibits a rustic theme that reflects the rural character of the region. Each village is oriented around a created "homestead" that links the village to the western heritage. Subtle differences in detailing give each village a different flavor. The villages are connected by pedestrian and horse trails. A pastoral scene of horses in paddocks greets everyone who enters Stillwater. (Figure 4.4) Expansive open spaces and golf-course views that simulate pastures visually separate the

behind. The majority of the parking, and the primary store entrance, face away from the Main Street.

Buyers' needs and desires also influence the nature of the community vision. There would be little value in creating a vision for a "western ranch" if the buyers were intent on living in urban row homes. The community designer

Figure 4.3 Small shops and restaurants bring life to the main street.

villages to reduce the perceived size of the 1,475-acre community.

The architecture of community features plays off the image of ranch and farm buildings. The information center is designed as a collection of smaller, ranch-style buildings that appear to be a barn and ranch house (Figure 4.5). The design of the community center and fire station, with large wood beams and rafters, stone columns, and simple vertical siding, contribute to the community vision. Stone walls visually anchor buildings to the side. This use of natural materials and a local architectural vernacular makes the vision believable.

The most successful visioning begins with a credible *community story*. The community story is simply a plausible history of a place. It expresses the roots of the community design

and helps define physical form and detail. Building a credible story is easier if the story is based on the location and character of the site and context. Community design and details can be evaluated to see whether they support, or degrade, the community story. Contrasting elements will seem out of place and diminish the value of the story.

The underlying community story for Autumn Lake is one of a small Wisconsin town that evolved over time. The market force behind this idea was that many people desired to live in the country, to have their own idyllic retreat. The reality is that most people cannot afford to purchase an estate in the country, so the thought was to give them an opportunity to purchase a part of a small village in the country. To be credible, the community had to exhibit

The most successful visioning begins with a credible community story.

Credit: Courtesy of DTJ Design.

Figure 4.4 Horses in pastures along the entry enhance the image of the Stillwater community.

Credit: Courtesy of DTJ Design.

Figure 4.5 The information center exhibits a western ranch architectural character.

the characteristics of a small Wisconsin town. Observation and research distilled small Wisconsin towns into three basic types: rail oriented, lake oriented, or farm oriented (Figure 4.6).

The rail village sprang from the small train station that was used to move goods and services from the country to more urban markets. When the village was closer to major cities, commuters also moved to the small village and took the train into the city to work. With the advent of the interstate highway system in the 1950s, the commercial hub around the station was diverted, if possible, to the highway interchange. Today, the small urban centers around the old train station are being redeveloped into unique communities.

The farm village had a similar history, with a rural crossroads instead of a train station being the primary driving force to settlement. As the village grew, a grange hall was built, and eventually a church and a school. A more formal village green grew near the crossroads of the town. As farmers retired, they moved into town. These small towns still dot the landscape in nearly every state.

The lake village began as a cluster of cottages along the lakeshore. A winding dirt road provided access to each cottage. Views of the lake dictated where the cottage was sited. As more people built cottages on the lake, a bait shop opened. The lake became a haven for summer fun. As cottages were winterized, people began to live at the lake year-round. Services were established, and the village grew.

A lake village dovetailed well with the opportunities and constraints of the site. A large, central area of poor soils and high water table suggested that a lake could be created on

site. The site is protected from the visual intrusion of standard subdivisions by an existing rail line and steep, wooded slopes. This layout was critical to establishing and maintaining the image of a small village in the country. Market demands indicated a need for a wide variety of housing types and price ranges, which support the notion of a village.

This combination became the cornerstone for the vision that is to become Autumn Lake. Creating a vision modeled after a lake village will capture the hearts and minds of many buyers. They will relate to spending summers at the lake with their family or growing up on a lake. They can image their children catching frogs along the shore, or watching fireworks explode over the lake on the Fourth of July. From this vision, design details begin to emerge.

To enhance the concept of the village, a study of some of Madison's most charming neighborhoods was completed (Figure 4.7). This study looked at street widths, tree lawns or terraces, home styles, architectural detailing, setbacks, and community amenities. The lessons learned from this study were implemented in the vision for Autumn Lake. Streets are narrow, respecting the pedestrian scale of the village; small, "found" open spaces are discovered when the grid of the neighborhood meets the road winding along the lake; setbacks relate to street type and traffic volumes, not lot size; and alley-loaded homes create a wonderful street character. The mayor and city council appreciate this expression of Madison's past and have embraced the concepts represented by the community plan and vision.

Amenities that support the varied events of small-town life are included in the vision

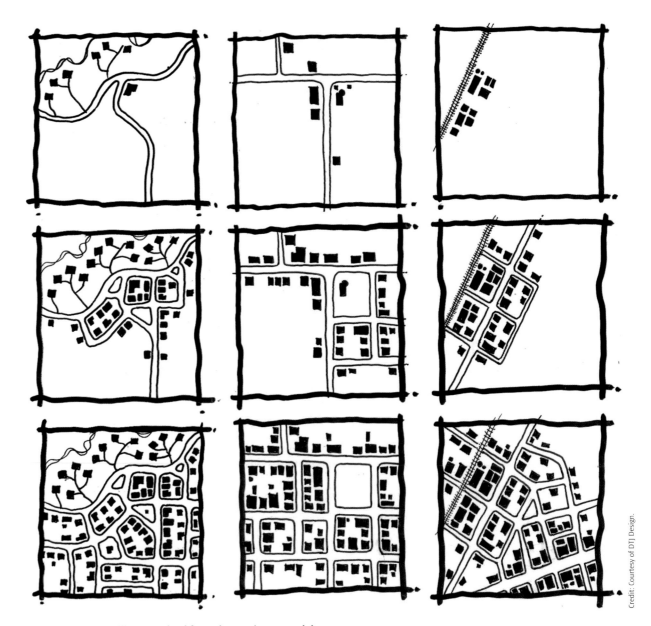

Figure 4.6 Small villages evolved from three primary models.

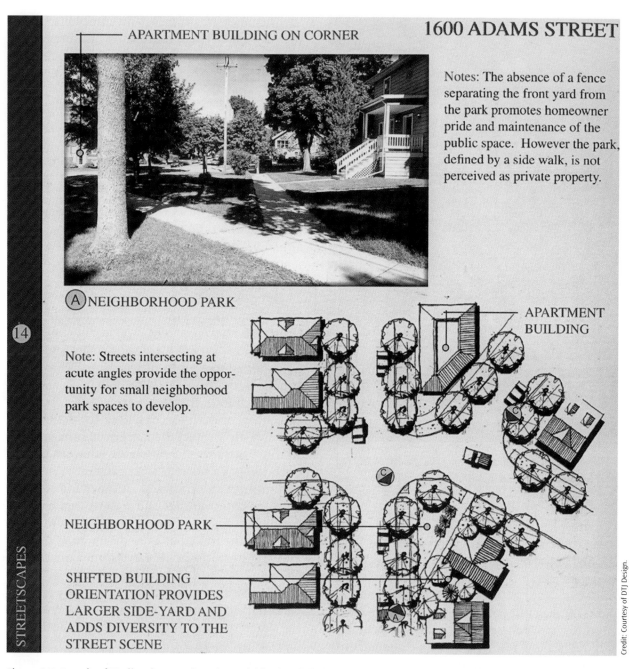

APARTMENT BUILDING ON CORNER

1600 ADAMS STREET

Notes: The absence of a fence separating the front yard from the park promotes homeowner pride and maintenance of the public space. However the park, defined by a side walk, is not perceived as private property.

Ⓐ NEIGHBORHOOD PARK

Note: Streets intersecting at acute angles provide the opportunity for small neighborhood park spaces to develop.

APARTMENT BUILDING

NEIGHBORHOOD PARK

SHIFTED BUILDING ORIENTATION PROVIDES LARGER SIDE-YARD AND ADDS DIVERSITY TO THE STREET SCENE

STREETSCAPES

⑭

Credit: Courtesy of DTJ Design.

Figure 4.7 A study of Madison's most charming neighborhoods helped create design standards for the Village at Autumn Lake.

Figure 4.8 At the Village at Autumn Lake the 4th of July is a time to come together as a community.

identity and encourages community life (Figures 4.9 and 4.10). Community buildings offer a valuable opportunity to establish and reinforce an architectural character for the community.

Amenities become an important connection between market desires and the community story. They are the places where community events happen. Careful thought must be given to understanding what amenities support the community events and thus the community story. Look to the opportunities and constraints of the site to suggest appropriate amenities. Using the existing site features can save money and have a more immediate impact.

It is also easier to create a credible vision for a community if it is set apart or protected from other development. The quality and character of conventional subdivisions may be detrimental to establishing a vision. When subdivisions are adjacent to poorly designed neighborhoods, transition areas, vegetation screening, or even fences and walls, may be necessary to protect the integrity of the vision. In those instances in which the adjacent neighborhood has a beneficial character, the new community vision should embrace the edge between communities and seek to create a seamless transition. Streets should connect, parks can be linked or even designed as one, and architecture should have some consistent elements.

In developing the community story and vision, the community designer must evaluate the visual quality of the adjacent uses and determine whether the existing character supports the evolving vision. Modifying the vision somewhat to blend the communities together

(Figure 4.8). A village green is designed to host a weekly farmers' market, a restaurant is located at the lake edge to serve hot chocolate to ice skaters in the winter time, the Easter egg hunt can occur at one of the neighborhood parks, and a craft fair can happen on the lakefront plaza. Open-space trails and detached sidewalks allow residents to move safely from one part of the community to the other. A community school adds to the community

Credit: Courtesy of DTJ Design.

Figure 4.9 A community school is designed to become a memorable civic building.

Figure 4.10 Community life is built around the little things that bring identity to the community.

may be appropriate. It is also necessary to determine whether the adjacent community property values have remained high, or have risen. These values indicate whether buyers appreciate the character of the adjacent community. If they do not, it would be wise to seek to differentiate the community.

Planning for a Community Vision

Creating a community vision demands a commitment to its success. Sufficient resources must be invested to create the vision on paper and to realize the vision in the field. To be effective, the vision must be well communi-

cated at each step of the process. A *summary vision document* effectively tells the community story and describes the vision in words and pictures. During the design phase, the community vision guides the planning and details. During the regulatory phase, the vision document communicates to the municipality what it can expect to see as the community is built. When properly executed, vision documents can expedite public acceptance and approvals for the development.

During the marketing and sales phase, the vision document helps buyers understand the vision and get excited about the community. They need to visualize being a part of the community. They need to know that this particular community is different, and special. During the construction phase, buyers need to see enough of the vision built to know that the vision will be implemented as promised. As people live in the community, they too need a commitment to the vision and should strive to build on what has been put in place.

Because the community vision benefits design, *entitlements*, and marketing, the cost of creating the vision should be allocated to each of those budgets. In some cases, the development's viability is directly related to the successful communication of a vision. Without it, there would be no development. The cost of constructing the vision should be budgeted to both community amenities and marketing. The initial budget analysis should include approximately 5 percent to 7 percent of the retail sales price of each home for vision creation and implementation. This budget would include the landscape and community amenities, and costs for refining the vision document as a significant marketing tool.

Although many developers take the conservative approach and do not account for premiums in their preliminary budgets and *pro forma analysis* (see Chapter Seven), community builders must account for the increased value the vision creates. This value can be represented either in higher base prices or by allocating a percentage of the expected premium to revenue. In time-sensitive pro forma analysis, sales pace should reflect the faster absorption expected from a well-designed community with a strong vision. The intangible value of easier approvals and a lasting legacy must also be considered. Easier approvals save time and money, and the legacy makes subsequent communities easier to entitle, build, and finance.

Controlling the Vision

To maintain the high values associated with a strong community vision, a *Home Owners Association (HOA)* should be established with the power to levy fees and contract the necessary maintenance work. Bylaws, *CC&Rs (codes, covenants and restrictions)*, or design guidelines must be developed that govern the operation of the HOA and set the standard for design and maintenance of all improvements. The bylaws will control membership in the association; the order, timing, and purpose of meetings; the power and duties of association officers; election procedures; and financial obligations and duties. The bylaws will also detail a procedure for amending the CCRs or design guidelines, and removal or replacement of officers or board members. Bylaws of the association are typically filed with the Secretary of State and are necessary to establish the power to assess dues. Association bylaws are a legal document and should be drafted by a competent attorney.

CC&Rs or design guidelines are created to control the standard of quality for proposed improvements and the maintenance of any existing improvements. They ensure that property owners will not have a detrimental impact on adjacent property values through poor maintenance or substandard design and construction. CC&Rs tend to concentrate on what homeowners may not do with their lot once they purchase a home. They cover restrictions to sites and buildings, fencing, satellite dishes and antennas, trash enclosures, snow removal, and proper lawn care. They also control unwanted activities, including nuisance pets, loud parties, inoperable vehicle storage, signs, boat and RV storage, and the like. CC&Rs give the authority to the Home Owners Association to monitor and control these activities and improvements.

In contrast to CC&Rs, which tend to focus on what cannot be done, design guidelines usually present a positive example of what should be done to achieve the original vision for the community. Well-conceived guidelines begin with a thorough discussion of the intent and value of the community vision. This helps homeowners understand why conformance to the guidelines is important to each property owner. These guidelines discuss the design approach for the community and describe the desired site planning, architecture, and landscape character. Specific design principles give additional meaning to the design guidelines.

A wide variety of design guidelines covers the basic issues of site planning, architecture, and landscape in varying detail. The least-restrictive guidelines encourage some conformance to the vision, but the results are limited by each property owner's desire to adhere to the vision. In some cases, property owners do not intend to diminish the vision; they just don't have the design ability or experience to make a positive contribution. More detailed design guidelines can have a positive influence when homeowners or designers aren't sure what to do. The following list suggests what a good set of design guidelines should include:

■ **Introduction.** The introduction should establish the purpose and intent of the guidelines. Much of the effort from the vision document can be used to communicate the intent of the community and provide a context for the design guidelines. The introduction will describe who needs to use the guidelines and for what purpose. It should include a section on how the guidelines are organized and how to resolve conflicts with other regulations. This section can also detail the submittal and review process, what drawings are required, the timing of review, who will make the final decision, and the procedure for appeal. Finally, this section should establish definitions for terms that are used in the guidelines.

■ **Site Planning Guidelines.** Site planning guidelines should, at a minimum, cover building siting, orientation and views, access, garages, and parking. The guidelines might also include how grading and drainage should be considered, and the treatment of decks, site walls, pools and spas, and large recreational elements such as tennis courts. An example might be that homes must be sited to work with the grade and minimize site grading and engineered slopes. Defining building envelopes within lots and access points to lots can begin to control the quality of building siting and will work together with the guidelines to enhance the visual quality of the community.

■ **Architecture Guidelines.** Much of the community character is created through building architecture. This architectural character has an impact on the success of the vision. Careful architectural guidance is vital to the realization of the vision. Architectural guidelines should include a discussion of building massing and form; roof forms and roof elements, including overhangs, *fascias*, and *soffits*; architectural elements, including window placement and groupings, doors, fireplaces and chimneys, trim details, and other elements of style, porches, and decks; exterior materials, colors, and lighting; and exterior building equipment, including air conditioners and communications equipment (Figure 4.11). Guidelines might suggest a minimum amount of masonry for the front elevation, or a minimum size for a useable front porch. What is important is that each requirement support the ideas outlined in the community vision.

- **Landscape Guidelines.** The quality of the landscape contributes to the successful implementation of the community vision. The landscape visually brings individual properties together, and it creates a wonderful setting for each home. The landscape and the architecture must work together to create a community character that is rooted in the site and environment. The landscape guidelines must cover how existing vegetation on site can be disturbed, and how it can be replaced (Figure 4.12). The guidelines should include acceptable plant species and sizes; plant locations and transitions; landscape treatment for specific site conditions—for example, along roadways, graded slopes, and adjacent to community amenities; fences and walls; landscape structures, such as trellises and gazebos; lighting; and installation.

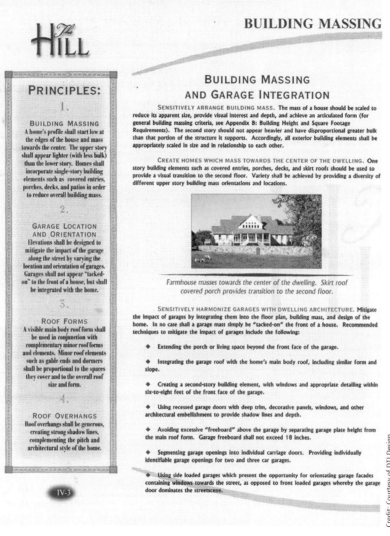

Figure 4.11 The Hill Architectural Guidelines preserve value by controlling major building elements.

The HILL

PRINCIPLES:

1.

PLANT QUANTITIES AND COVERAGE
Promote the use of introduced plant materials which supplement and harmonize with existing native plant species.

2.

LANDSCAPE INTEGRATION BETWEEN LOTS
Create a cohesive "flowing" relationship between lots. Landscape designs emphasizing and delineating lot lines shall not be permitted.

3.

LANDSCAPE INTEGRATION ADJACENT TO OPEN SPACE
Create a unified landscape image between private lots and common open space. Introduced plants shall harmonize with adjacent open space areas and existing natural landscapes. Plants shall be arranged on private lots to mingle with neighboring natural open space areas, resulting in a soft blending of introduced and native vegetation.

V-3

LANDSCAPE QUANTITIES,

PLANT QUANTITIES, COVERAGE, AND LOCATION

ZONE 1: CREATE A WOODED HAVEN AROUND THE HOME DESIGNED TO PRO-MOTE A SECLUDED ENVIRONMENT WHICH GRADUALLY TRANSITIONS TO LOW PRAIRIE GRASSLANDS. Zone 1 landscapes shall be planted with species contained on the Plant Association List, (Appendix A), according to the following requirements:

◆ Trees - Zone 1 shall contain a minimum of 12 trees clustered within the building envelope. A minimum of eight of the required trees shall be planted within the front yard area. Trees shall be a mix of deciduous species. Trees shall be planted in odd number clustered in groups and appropriately spaced per species type.

◆ Irrigated Turf Grass - Zone 1 may contain irrigated turf grass. Turf grass shall not cover more than 65 percent of the total area of Zone 1.

Within Zone 1 trees are clustered close to the house and irrigated turf grass is permitted.

ZONE 2: CREATE A TRANSITIONAL AREA BETWEEN ORNAMENTAL ZONE 1 AND NATIVE ZONE 3 COMPOSED OF WOODY SHRUBS AND GRASSES. Zone 2 landscapes shall be planted with species contained on the Recommended Plant Association List, according to the following requirements:

◆ Shrubs - Approximately 30-40 percent of the total area of Zone 2 shall be covered with shrubs planted in informal drifts. Shrub coverage shall be based upon the following criteria:

• small shrubs: occupy nine square feet
• medium shrubs: occupy 16 square feet
• large shrubs: occupy 25-32 square feet

◆ Native Grassland Seed Mix - Zone 2 shall be planted with a native grassland seed mix based on a ratio of 16 pounds of seed mix per acre.

Woody shrubs and grasses provide a transition between manicured plantings and natural prairie grasslands.

Credit: Courtesy of DTJ Design.

Figure 4.12 Landscape Guidelines help control the image of the community.

Design guidelines should be informative, illustrative, and fun to read. They should be a part of the visioning package and should help communicate the vision for the community to regulators, buyers, and other builders. Design guidelines increase the comfort level of review agencies that the community will meet a high level of design. They preserve value for the builder and the home buyers. The builder knows that the investment in community visioning will be enhanced by the efforts of the homeowners, and the homeowners know that their investment in the design and quality of their homes will be only positively affected by what their neighbors build.

The design guidelines for Tallyn's Reach took a fun and unique approach to design regulation. The vision for Tallyn's Reach is an old farmstead founded along the stagecoach trail from Kansas City to Denver. This vision suggests a history of Colorado and brings life to the community. The design guidelines were written as a design sourcebook, providing builder and developers with inspiration to create something special. The guidelines are hosted by Blanche, a tour guide who provides the reader with helpful tips along the journey (Figure 4.13). The introduction features postcards from make-believe visitors to Tallyn's Reach who write of the wonders of what they have seen.

The guidelines themselves present both desirable and undesirable architectural images. They explain why a style fits the Colorado vernacular, and how to organize buildings along a street. The guidelines are designed to promote design flexibility. There are not rigid rules of what to do; however, there are design principles and criteria that must be respected.

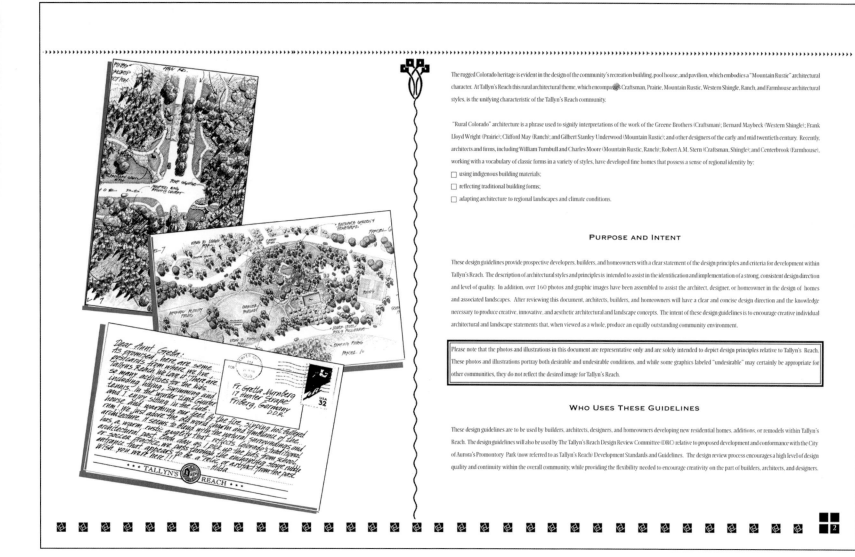

The rugged Colorado heritage is evident in the design of the community's recreation building, pool house, and pavilion, which embodies a "Mountain Rustic" architectural character. At Tallyn's Reach this rural architectural theme, which encompasses Craftsman, Prairie, Mountain Rustic, Western Shingle, Ranch, and Farmhouse architectural styles, is the unifying characteristic of the Tallyn's Reach community.

"Rural Colorado" architecture is a phrase used to signify interpretations of the work of the Greene Brothers (Craftsman); Bernard Maybeck (Western Shingle); Frank Lloyd Wright (Prairie); Clifford May (Ranch); and Gilbert Stanley Underwood (Mountain Rustic); and other designers of the early and mid twentieth century. Recently, architects and firms, including William Turnbull and Charles Moore (Mountain Rustic, Ranch); Robert A.M. Stern (Craftsman, Shingle); and Centerbrook (Farmhouse), working with a vocabulary of classic forms in a variety of styles, have developed fine homes that possess a sense of regional identity by:

☐ using indigenous building materials;

☐ reflecting traditional building forms;

☐ adapting architecture to regional landscapes and climate conditions.

PURPOSE AND INTENT

These design guidelines provide prospective developers, builders, and homeowners with a clear statement of the design principles and criteria for development within Tallyn's Reach. The description of architectural styles and principles is intended to assist in the identification and implementation of a strong, consistent design direction and level of quality. In addition, over 160 photos and graphic images have been assembled to assist the architect, designer, or homeowner in the design of homes and associated landscapes. After reviewing this document, architects, builders, and homeowners will have a clear and concise design direction and the knowledge necessary to produce creative, innovative, and aesthetic architectural and landscape concepts. The intent of these design guidelines is to encourage creative individual architectural and landscape statements that, when viewed as a whole, produce an equally outstanding community environment.

Please note that the photos and illustrations in this document are representative only and are solely intended to depict design principles relative to Tallyn's Reach. These photos and illustrations portray both desirable and undesirable conditions, and while some graphics labeled "undesirable" may certainly be appropriate for other communities, they do not reflect the desired image for Tallyn's Reach.

WHO USES THESE GUIDELINES

These design guidelines are to be used by builders, architects, designers, and homeowners developing new residential homes, additions, or remodels within Tallyn's Reach. The design guidelines will also be used by The Tallyn's Reach Design Review Committee (DRC) relative to proposed development and conformance with the City of Aurora's Promontory Park (now referred to as Tallyn's Reach) Development Standards and Guidelines. The design review process encourages a high level of design quality and continuity within the overall community, while providing the flexibility needed to encourage creativity on the part of builders, architects, and designers.

Figure 4.13 Design guidelines should be informative and fun to read.

(Figure 4.14) This flexibility has allowed the architectural control committee and the developer to make decisions based on current market conditions. Examples help the reader fully understand what is expected. Together, principles, examples, and design criteria have resulted in a wonderful community. (Figure 4.15)

To repeat, builders and developers who invest the time and money in creating a memorable vision for a community will experience greater public acceptance both during the approval process and the marketing of the project, with a substantial return on investment. They will begin to change the public's perception of builders to an image of creative companies interested in people's values and the quality of community life. This perception returns dividends for every community the builder creates. Fully realizing a vision creates a legacy for the builder and enduring value for the buyer.

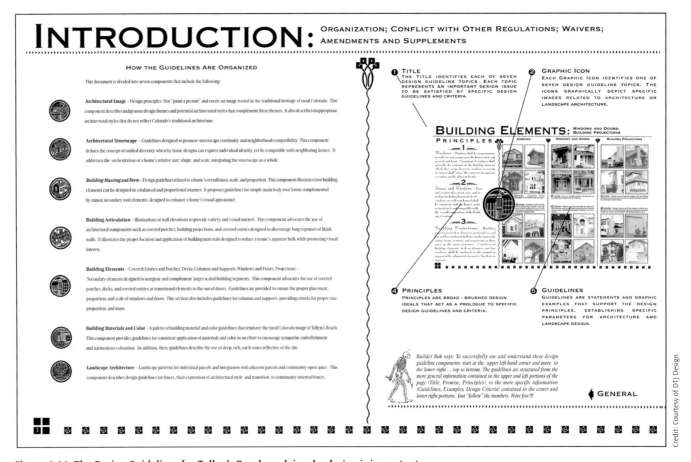

Figure 4.14 The Design Guidelines for Tallyn's Reach explain why design is important.

Figure 4.15 The Tallyn's Reach Design Guidelines have helped create quality production builder architecture.

CHAPTER 5
Community Design

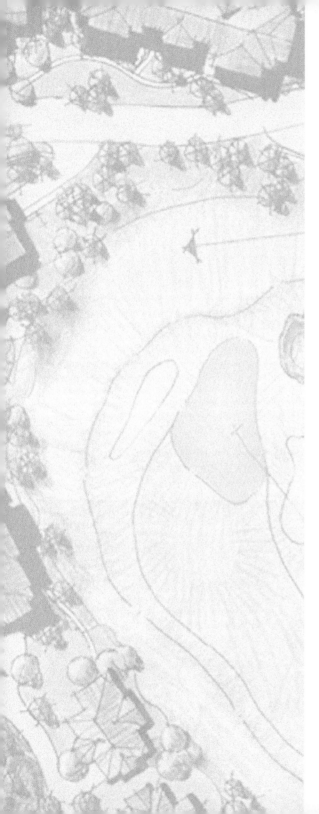

The goal of community design is to create wonderful places for people to live, to work, to shop, and to play. These places can be simple and inexpensive. They can be highly detailed, composed of rich materials and textures. They can be quiet places for reflection and contemplation, or energized places where people can revel in activity. Places may be clear and straightforward, or they may be full of surprise and delight. However these places are articulated, the purpose is to touch users in some positive way. They might elicit a smile at a bird dancing in the trees, a memory of childhood days at the croak of a bullfrog in the pond, or even joy at the play of children in the park.

Designing community is more than evaluating each of the elements of a site analysis or achieving the maximum number of units on the land. It goes beyond a simple checklist of what should be included in the community. In short, it is more than a house on a street. Successful community design is the result of a passion for community, a process that generates great ideas and a development pattern that responds to site context.

Passion for Community

Community is more than the physical manifestation of development. It is more than the bricks and sticks, tangible and concrete. Successful community design relies on an expanded notion of community. The heart of the community comes from the people within. It is necessary to think of community in terms of the connections made between people. Value is created when these connections, or *community life,* becomes an integral part of the community design. The purpose of the physical design is to create places for the events in people's lives to happen.

A community of friends might share a property line or a Saturday night BBQ. A community of friends might be the people we wave to each morning as we grab the paper from the driveway, or the people we talk to from the sidewalk on an evening stroll. We can design our streets and homes to encourage these brief, but important, social interactions. We can create intimate spaces within the neighborhood to give identity to a cluster of homes. We can incorporate small gathering places throughout the community. Building community creates places that reflect buyers' varied lifestyles, needs, and aspirations (Figure 5.1).

A community of neighbors might share a larger, common interest. Children might compete together on the swim team or soccer field. Neighbors might enjoy the same neighborhood park. The play field might be designed to accommodate a neighborhood softball game, or the community might include a school at which people come together to watch sports,

concerts, or plays. The traditional recreation center can be expanded to allow a daycare or neighborhood deli. The community should be designed to appeal to the individual walker and jogger as well as the sports team (Figure 5.2). The neighborhood might establish a babysitting co-op, or sponsor an Easter egg hunt, a community picnic, or a children's fishing tournament (Figure 5.3). The community builder can support events that define the places it builds.

A community of citizens might come together to watch the fireworks over the lake on the Fourth of July. These members might come together to shop at the farmer's market, boat on the lake, or use the walking and biking trails. Citizens connect across neighborhood boundaries and share in the pride of where they live. Similarities and differences are celebrated through the diversity of housing types and price ranges, under an umbrella of consistent design elements. Homes may exhibit similar architectural elements or materials, and

Figure 5.1 Providing places for recreation enhances the sense of community.

Figure 5.2 Sports teams often bring families from various parts of the community together.

Figure 5.3 Parks become great places for events to happen.

landscape form and texture may visually bring the community together. The community builder might create a community foundation intent on bringing art and culture to the residents, or the builder might develop a community Intranet.

These events become central to the buyers' perception of the community and can be the deciding factor in any purchase decision. For the most part, these events are not expensive to implement. They can be an outgrowth of the marketing efforts or the responsibility of a community concierge hired by the builder as the community develops. Much of the work is organizational, and once it has been incorporated into one community, the cost of implementation is much less for subsequent communities. These value-added community events and programs can become a builder's hallmark, creating a following and loyalty among home buyers.

Rob Bowman, of Charter Homes, is such a builder. Rob is active in developing creative ideas to bring residents and potential buyers together. At one event, Rob and his team organized a barn dance, complete with a BBQ and mechanical bull. At another, Charter Homes sponsored a free outdoor movie night at the community facility, showing the movie *Grease*, preceded by face painting, balloon sculpting, hula-hoop contests, and a tour of finished model homes. Snacks were available for purchase, and the proceeds were donated to the American Heart Association. Such events are memorable in the minds of the homeowners and communicate that the community is a special place.

With the increased focus on community life, loyal home buyers become an important part of the community marketing. Satisfied buyers are an effective endorsement of the community. The community builder can host community parties for existing homeowners and encourage them to invite several of their friends. The parties can be simple BBQs or box lunches; the purpose is to show the community, amenities, and community life to potential buyers. In addition to marketing the community, these connections create a stronger bond among homeowners. Through these events, the community builder demonstrates a caring for the residents, who, in turn, demonstrate a greater stewardship for each other and the community.

Community Design Process

Great community design is born in a process that encourages innovation, respect for every member of the development team, and sensitivity to the site context. As the community story begins to evolve from the site analysis, market research, and visioning, the entire development team should establish *design drivers*, or goals, that will guide conceptual and final design. These design drivers help focus design decisions that support the community vision. Embedded within each design goal should be specific design strategies that will help achieve that goal.

Design drivers must respond to the site context and enhance the community story. The goals should be clear and concise. The design strategies should be easily implemented. The following design goals and strategies helped mold the plan for a recent community in Colorado.

Goal #1: Reinforce the Colorado lifestyle.
Generally, the people living along the Colorado Front Range are young, well-educated, and recreation oriented. They appreciate the proximity to the mountains and will invest in a community and home that visually, and literally, supports that image.

Design Strategies
- Provide a fine texture of open space throughout the community.
- Create active open space within a three-minute walk of any home.
- Provide visual open space along major roadways.
- Develop a recreation facility as the heart of the community.
- Maintain mountain views from public parks and circulation.

Goal #2: Create a memorable drive home. The image of the community must extend beyond the entry feature. One way to achieve that extended image is to create a sequence of places that visually connect the drive from the entry to various parts of the community. These places act as memory points that enhance the community story or support the community image.

Design Strategies
- Take advantage of views to parks, mountains, and lakes.
- Pass through open space along the drive.
- Establish visual diversity along the drive.

Goal #3: Strengthen the community through diversity. It is unlikely that all price ranges and product types will suffer equally during depressed market conditions. Communities that exhibit a variety of housing product and price range are more stable and better able to withstand the rise and fall of the local economy. This variety preserves housing values.

Design Strategies
- Enhance visual interest through smaller clusters of different land uses, including attached residential and nonresidential uses.
- Respond to market demand by offering a variety of home types and price ranges.

In addition to defining a design direction, design drivers begin to communicate to the municipality and the public a thoughtful process that links site context to final design. This connection helps these populations understand why the community plan looks like it does, and it can result in faster approvals and fewer plan modifications than otherwise might occur as part of the public-approval process. This step can also facilitate a discussion of the municipality goals, which can be integrated into the design drivers. As the community design achieves the municipality's goals, trust is built between the builder and the municipality.

An added benefit is that a well-conceived and well-designed community increases the level of expectation on the part of the public-review agencies, which essentially "raises the bar" on acceptable community design. This effect reduces the chance a poor-quality builder will be able to build a substandard community, compete on the basis of price alone, and contribute to the public backlash

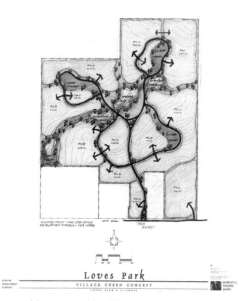

Figure 5.4 This concept idea illustrates smaller, neighborhood-oriented open spaces as the primary organizing element.

Figure 5.5 This concept idea illustrates a centrally located open space as the primary organizing element.

against sprawl. Excellent architecture and community design eases the oft-times tough approval process, saving time and money. Quality design is not mutually exclusive of affordability. Home sizes may be somewhat smaller, and architectural details may be simpler; however, the benefits of quality design can be achieved at all price ranges.

Concept Ideas

Effective community design begins with a strong thought, or idea. The *concept idea* provides structure to the plan, a framework on which to drape details. To minimize the tendency to delve into the details too quickly, concept ideas should be formed at a large scale on a small piece of paper. This approach forces the designer to focus only on the major components of the community: amenities, open space and trails, major circulation, and land use. This approach also allows the design team to generate a large number of concept ideas in a short time. These concept ideas can become the nucleus of the community story (Figures 5.4 and 5.5).

The concept ideas must then be evaluated with respect to sensitivity to the site context, the market, relative developable area, the community story, and sales and marketing advantages and disadvantages. The pros and cons of each plan should be listed in a summary of the plans and referred to as the design team evaluates each option. Several concept ideas may warrant further investigation and should be developed into more detailed concept-plan alternatives. As with the community visioning and design drivers, the concept ideas should be used to guide more detailed design decisions throughout the process.

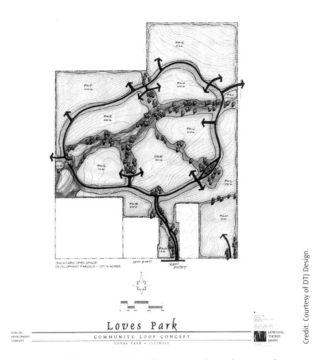

Figure 5.6 This concept idea illustrates a large loop road as the primary organizing element.

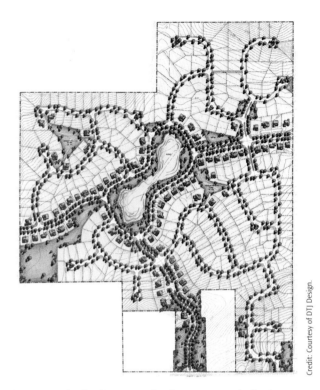

Figure 5.7 The final concept plan incorporates the best features of the concept ideas.

As concept ideas are being developed, generating as many alternatives as possible is important. Several individuals initially working in isolation or through a group brainstorming session can accomplish this goal. Whichever method yields the most distinctly different concept ideas is the most appropriate. How the initial ideas are generated is not as important as the process used to evaluate them. The entire development team, including the community design team, engineers, sales and marketing people, construction management, and the builder/developer, must evaluate each idea against the design drivers established earlier and each member's own area of expertise. The discussion resulting from this design review often leads to additional ideas, a blending of ideas, or a refinement of one approach. The community designer must facilitate this discussion and ensure that the concept ideas do not stray too far from the design goals, and that the chosen concept idea truly exhibits a strong community story or theme (Figure 5.6 and Figure 5.7). To ensure that the concept ideas remain relevant to the market, and are functional and cost effective, is incumbent on the community designer.

Elements of Community

As the design team refines a chosen concept idea, several community elements emerge to give the community character. The community designer's palette includes streets, buildings, landscape and earth forms, and open spaces. How developers manipulate those elements creates texture, massing, contrast, and color. Participants can experience the composition dynamically, as they move through the community, or statically, as they enjoy one element at a time. The designer uses these community elements to define spaces and evoke emotions to create memorable places.

Texture. The texture of the community is controlled primarily by the definition of land use and open space. A finer texture is visually more interesting, reduces the perception of monotonous density (as it applies to housing types), and increases value. Community value is increased as the result of faster absorption through multiple home types, higher prices resulting from a more pleasing street scene, and maximized edge conditions on open space.

A finer texture of land uses is a combination of building types (various housing types and nonresidential buildings), lot sizes and coverage, and open space (Figure 5.8). In the

Credit: Courtesy of DTJ Design.

Figure 5.8 Nonresidential buildings can provide a variety of texture in the community design.

simplest form of texture, distinct housing blocks begin to break down the scale of the community into more readily perceived neighborhoods. As the community texture becomes more complex, the neighborhood blocks may be divided into street segments of different land uses or housing types. At the smallest scale, lot sizes and housing types may vary on individual side-by-side lots along even the smallest street.

Community texture is also influenced by the use of various materials for buildings and street furniture. Explore using a variety of brick or stone in combination with siding, shingles, or stucco for alternate elevations. The material choice should reflect the site context and community story, or regional theme. Street furniture, such as stop signs, street signs, light poles, information signs, benches, and mailboxes, also adds to the texture of the community. The design and placement of these elements should also contribute to the overall character of the community.

A finer texture of open space brings amenities in contact with more people. Creating a greater number of smaller open spaces brings these amenities close to home and makes them more accessible. Larger, community open spaces continue to serve larger recreation functions. Together, the open spaces provide residents with choices that serve their immediate need. Small children may play in the open space close to home, while older children and adults may be drawn to the larger, community open spaces.

Landscape and hardscape (hardscape is the plazas, walkways, and hard-surface gathering areas within the community) contribute to the texture of the community. Planting can create a rhythm along the street, identify key site locations and amenities, and create a human scale to the community. Plazas and walkways highlight places within the community, create places for events to happen, and connect the community. These elements all combine to create community texture.

Massing. Variation in building mass relates not only to the type of housing but also to the quality of the visual environment. People react negatively to repetition of the same thing, and this is especially true for buildings. At a larger scale, too much of the same building design is confusing, unimaginative, and boring. Such repetition does not allow for the pride of ownership that comes from personalizing residences.

At a smaller scale, identical building massing ignores the opportunity to create *street music* that comes with the interplay of one- and two-story building mass, and gables that either front or face perpendicular to the street. By predesignating the orientation and massing for each lot, a visual rhythm can be established that builds and falls as the viewer moves through the community (Figure 5.9). This rhythm can create quiet places along the street or build to a crescendo at key locations within the community.

Building massing can also help organize the community. As residents approach the perceived "heart" of the community, building intensity might increase. Higher intensity nodes can surround key amenity places within the community. These places may be a village square, a community park, a major intersection, or even a recreation center. The heart of the community might also be a commercial

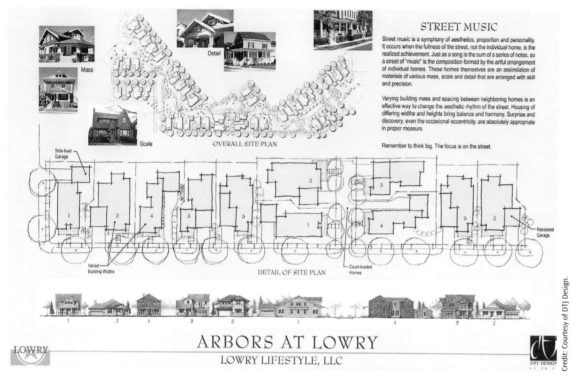

Figure 5.9 The rhythm of buildings creates street music.

core, similar to Country Club Plaza in Kansas City, which was discussed in Chapter 1.

Contrast and Color. Contrast between developed versus open areas, and between housing types, enhances the diversity found within a well-designed community. Contrast in housing design, type, and size gives each cluster a stronger identity, which helps residents feel connected to the larger community.

Color can be also be used to give individual identity to homes within the neighborhood (Figure 5.10). Color increases visual diversity, while a similar color palette can visually unify a neighborhood. Consistency, with some

building colors accented with various door and trim colors, can bring excitement to the community while ensuring compatibility. As with massing, color can also be used to highlight key locations within a community. A gradual shift in color intensity can signal the approach to a special community feature. Color applications should also extend to the landscape, where vivid color and a finer plant texture will celebrate special places within the community.

Community Design Strategies

Over the years, community design strategies have emerged that can be categorized into six

Figure 5.10 Color can be used to create individuality for each home.

major community types. These types include the following:

- Open-space communities
- Amenity-based communities
- Traditional neighborhood developments (TNDs)
- Blended communities
- Suburban and urban mixed-use communities
- Urban infill communities

Each type of community has a place within the context of site opportunities, constraints, and market desires. Generally, the communi-

ties respond to site location, from rural, to suburban, to urban communities. The first four community design types are generally found in suburban locations, while the final two are typically found in more urban locations.

This transition in intensity is referred to as the *rural to urban transect*, in which building typology and community design pattern vary depending on the location of the community. The transect is divided into six primary categories, two representing rural character, two representing suburban neighborhood zones, and two representing urban zones. Within each zone, there are variations in street patterns and cross-sections, building forms, relationship to the environment, and investment in public infrastructure. Each variation provides for a variety of housing types and price ranges to appeal to the broadest possible market.

In rural and suburban areas, where greenfield development predominates, development patterns are usually looser to accommodate varied terrain, and building massing is lower or clustered to respect the scale of the countryside. In urban areas, densities are higher, building massing is greater, and public open spaces take on a special prominence.

Pressure to codify the transect as a development tool is growing in cities across the country. The intent is to create a code that dictates character of place as an alternative to conventional zoning. Community builders should carefully review the potential impact of these codes to ensure they do not limit well-designed communities.

Open-Space Community Design

As the name *open-space community design* implies, the dominant characteristic of this community type is open space. Usually, this open space is composed of natural areas that exist on the site; however, on a site with few natural features, the open space may need to be enhanced. Large stands of mature vegetation, streams or creeks, wetlands, steep slopes or ravines, and lakes and ponds are some of the site features that can characterize the community. The design strategy incorporates these open spaces as natural amenities and supplements them with man-made open-space fea-

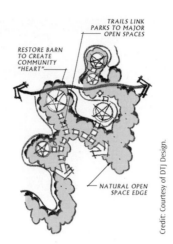

RESTORE BARN TO CREATE COMMUNITY "HEART"

TRAILS LINK PARKS TO MAJOR OPEN SPACES

NATURAL OPEN SPACE EDGE

Credit: Courtesy of DTJ Design.

Figure 5.11 A concept idea for an open-space community.

tures (Figure 5.11). The open spaces can be linked together with hard or soft trails to form a backbone to the community design.

In some open-space communities, the open space is the sole amenity. The natural areas may be celebrated with placards that describe the environmental benefit of the feature, or that identify the common and scientific names of trees and other plants. Boardwalks may wind through the marsh or wetland, allowing residents to view the wildlife teeming within. Crushed stone, wood-chip mulch, or paved trails encourage people to get out of their cars and enjoy the natural features. In other communities, open-space areas are designed as parks, with playgrounds and open play fields. The heavy reliance on the conservation of natural features found in most open-space communities should become part of the community story and an integral part of the marketing.

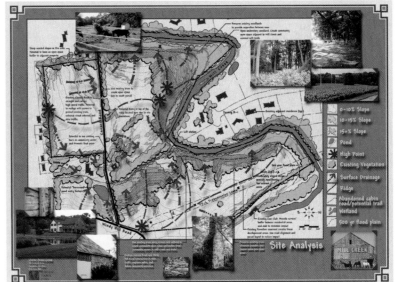

Figure 5.12 A site analysis identified the most important site features.

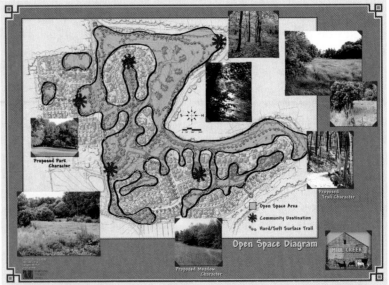

Figure 5.13 The open-space concept was in response to the open-space features of the site.

MILL CREEK

Lancaster, Pennsylvania

In its undeveloped state, the Mill Creek site was typical of many central Pennsylvania farms. Gently rolling hills, bisected by a small creek emptying into a larger stream, defined the edge of the property. The creek flowed slowly through wetland areas that filtered the water before it reached the creek. The stream was crystal clear, with the stone bottom visible through about two feet of water. On the steeper slope adjacent to the stream, hardwood forests had grown. The flatter hilltops were farmed, with small, isolated stands of trees remaining around rock outcrops. An existing *bank barn* (a barn set into the side of the hill, or bank) a cottage ruin found in the trees, and a small pump house were the only structures on the site. A row of large trees ran along side the existing country lane that provided access to the site.

The community design for Mill Creek responds to these natural features in several important ways (Figure 5.12). The country lane was realigned south so that roadway expansion would not damage the row of large trees. Preserving these trees along the roadway reinforces the notion that Mill Creek is an open-space community. The entry was located along the creek, where it intersected with the country lane, thus distinguishing the entry experience for all residents. The creek was preserved, and additional wetlands were created by the establishment of storm-water ponds near the creek. These areas were planted with wetland vegetation, which essentially cleans run-off before it enters the creek. The effect is a major open space link that connects the entry with the stream corridor to the north (Figure 5.13).

The bank barn was restored, creating a literal expression of the site's history, and a community facility was constructed adjacent to the barn. Together, these elements form the heart of the community and establish an indigenous character at the main entry. Reminiscent of early advertisements, this character was further enhanced by painting the community name on the stone end of the barn (Figure 5.14). This unique entry statement replaces the typical wall and sign found at the entry to many new communities. The main level of the community facility houses a community room, suitable for meetings or parties, while the lower, walkout level is home to a country store that offers coffee and pastries as well as gift baskets and sundries. Residents can walk to the country store each morning to read the paper, visit with friends, or enjoy the wildlife along the creek. Importantly, the country store is visible from the existing country lane, which allows passing traffic an opportunity to also enjoy the setting and purchase goods for sale. The restored barn has a large open area that will host large parties or community dances.

Townhomes across the creek from the main entry step up the hill, using retaining walls and walkout units to save trees (Figure 5.15). Units facing the main street are rear-loaded, eliminating the need for driveway curb cuts along the street. Large street trees were planted to create the image of the buildings gently placed in the landscape. Across the street to the north, cluster single-family homes tuck into the trees (Figure 5.16). Again, garages are set back from the front facade of the home, allowing the home architecture to establish the street character. Neighborhood play areas and landscaped courts give children a place to play and adults a place to relax.

Along a heavily treed ridge, estate single-family homes are carefully sited to minimize disturbance of the trees and slope. Building envelopes have been defined, restricting tree clearing and preserving privacy between homes. A narrow, private drive winds down the hill, avoiding large specimen trees while providing access. In the former fields, clusters of duplex units are arranged around a community garden. This garden is the centerpiece of the amenity for the empty-nester buyers, and it will

Figure 5.14 The restored barn and community building are the heart of the new community.

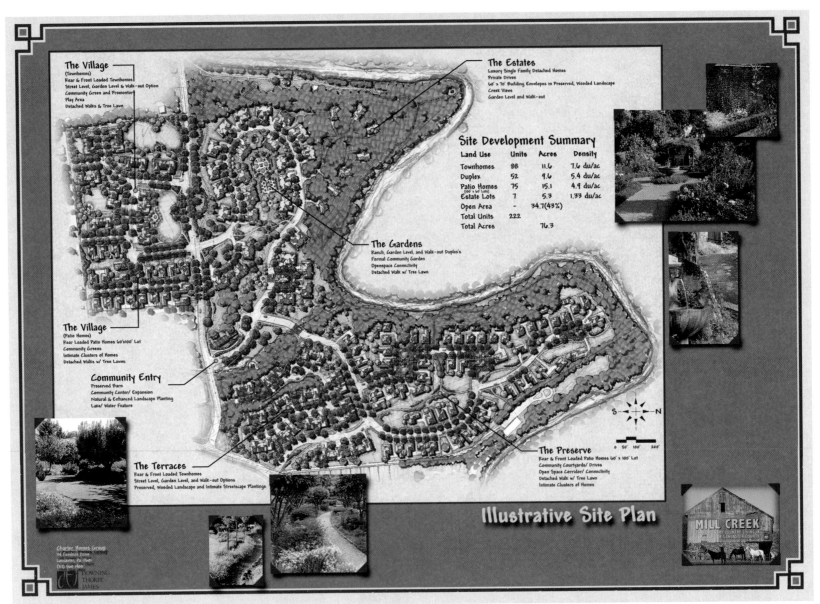

The Village
(Townhomes)
Rear & Front Loaded Townhomes
Street Level, Garden Level & Walk-out Option
Community Green and Promontory
Play Area
Detached Walks & Tree Lawn

The Estates
Luxury Single Family Detached Homes
Private Drives
60' x 70' Building Envelopes in Preserved, Wooded Landscape
Creek Views
Garden Level and Walk-out

The Gardens
Ranch, Garden Level, and Walk-out Duplex's
Formal Community Garden
Openspace Connectivity
Detached Walk w/ Tree Lawn

The Village
(Patio Homes)
Rear Loaded Patio Homes 60'x100' Lot
Community Greens
Intimate Clusters of Homes
Detached Walks w/ Tree Lawns

Community Entry
Preserved Barn
Community Center/ Expansion
Natural & Enhanced Landscape Planting
Lake/ Water Feature

The Terraces
Rear & Front Loaded Townhomes
Street Level, Garden Level, and Walk-out Options
Preserved, Wooded Landscape and Intimate Streetscape Plantings.

The Preserve
Rear & Front Loaded Patio Homes 60' x 100' Lot
Community Courtyards/ Drives
Open Space Corridor/ Connectivity
Detached Walk w/ Tree Lawn
Intimate Clusters of Homes

Site Development Summary

Land Use	Units	Acres	Density
Townhomes	88	11.6	7.6 du/ac
Duplex	52	9.6	5.4 du/ac
Patio Homes (60' x 60' Lots)	75	15.1	4.9 du/ac
Estate Lots	7	5.3	1.33 du/ac
Open Area	-	34.7 (43%)	
Total Units	222		
Total Acres		76.3	

Illustrative Site Plan

Charter Homes Group
116 Fossbire Drive
Lancaster, Pa 17601
(717) 560-1600

DOWNING
THORPE
JAMES

MILL CREEK
COUNTRY LIVING IN
LANCASTER COUNTY

Figure 5.15 The site plan for Mill Creek reflects the opportunities discovered in the site analysis.

be anchored by a formal garden area with a fountain or arbor gate. Across the country lane to the south, another field is developed into a central park with townhome and single-family homes clustered around the park. A small open space with a play structure softens the edge to the adjacent neighborhood.

Detached concrete sidewalks and a soft trail connect the barn and community building to the creek, through the trees along the stream, and across the road to the parks. It is possible to walk from nearly each home in the community to the community building and cross no more than two roads. Along the way, walkers can enjoy the active recreation of the parks or the quiet solitude of the trees. They can mingle with their neighbors or watch the geese and goslings play in the water. There are open-space opportunities for everyone.

The West Lampeter Township and Lancaster County officials also played an important role in the development of Mill Creek. By adopting a new ordinance, the officials allowed the developer to build narrower roads and much smaller lots than previously approved. The higher densities (222 units on 76 acres, or three times the typical density) gave the builder incentive to invest in the community infrastructure, and the narrower roads reduced the amount of site disturbance and gave the community a human scale. Cars take the back seat to pedestrians in Mill Creek.

In an area dominated by large lot subdivisions, Mill Creek has performed very well. Buyers have enthusiastically responded to the conservation ethic and mix of housing types. Mill Creek has enjoyed tremendous presale activity in a market that typically does not purchase until the home is built. More than 22 homes covering all housing types were presold.

Figure 5.16 As many homes as possible are nestled into the trees and garages are set back from the front elevation.

Amenity-Based Community Design

At the heart of an *amenity-based community* is a dramatic recreation amenity that is perceived throughout the entire community. In the Southeast, such an amenity might be a marina and waterways; in the West, it might be an elaborate tennis or swim center; or in the mountain region, it might be a ski run. For many states, the most popular amenity is golf. Golf-course communities meet the needs of many golf enthusiasts and reflect a large number of buyers who are willing to pay more to live on the manicured open space, separate from viewing the sport itself (Figure 5.17). Lot premiums along the best private courses can be well over one hundred thousand dollars; for many public courses, lot premiums are measured in the tens of thousands of dollars.

The linear nature of a golf course makes it possible to extend the golf experience from the center of the community (the clubhouse) in all directions to the edges and entries. Roads can touch the course in key locations to reinforce the golf image in the minds of residents as they move throughout the community. From these glimpses at golf, lot values away from the course are also increased. The key is to balance the lot frontage on the course with the need to extend the golf image into the community, while preserving a great experience for the golfer.

The most common approach to designing a golf community is to establish the clubhouse in a dramatic part of the site. This setting creates visual interest in the course by establishing a memorable view, and it can create value along the drive to the clubhouse. From that point, two returning nines provide significant golf-course frontage, minimize the number of road crossings, give the golfer a break at the club-

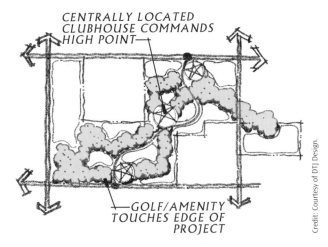

Figure 5.17 An amenity-based concept idea.

house between nines, and maximize the number of rounds that can be played on any given day. To alleviate the feeling of playing in a "canyon of homes," some holes may be placed side-by-side, which creates a larger open space. Side-by side golf holes reduces the linear frontage of homes on the golf course which can reduce the premiums, however, this is offset by the reduced amount of land required for holes that are adjacent to each other.

In some markets (resort, high-end residential), community value can be increased by clustering complementary land uses in a village setting adjacent to the clubhouse. Recreation centers, boutique shopping, spas, and conference and meeting rooms are synergistic uses that bring more people to the hub of the community. The higher activity level contributes to community life and expands the draw of the golf experience. The buildings that house these activities can be designed to support, or even create, the community image and story.

LEGACY RIDGE

Westminster, Colorado

With panoramic views of the Colorado Front Range, the 735-acre site that was to become the Legacy Ridge Golf Course Community was a diverse parcel of land. High ridges looked down on gentle valleys punctuated with idyllic ponds and isolated wetlands. Large cottonwood trees grew alongside the Farmers Highline Canal, a regional irrigation ditch that brings water from the mountains through the Denver metropolitan area, to farmers on the high plains. Owned by two families for generations, the land was perfectly suited for a high-end public golf course.

In an effort to increase the amount of higher-end housing within the city, municipal officials were motivated to work with the landowners to facilitate a golf-course community. The city took it upon itself to invest in a golf-feasibility study and preliminary land planning to illustrate to the property owners the value of working together to create a new golf community. This initial investment has paid dividends many times over through spectacular homes on very desirable lots. In 2001, golf-course lot premiums were approximately $80,000, with an additional $50,000 premium attached to lots with mountain views. The city of Westminster has been very successful in attracting some of the highest-priced homes in the northern Denver metropolitan region.

Public and Private Goals Achieved at Legacy Ridge

- Provide visibility to the golf course from all adjacent roadways.
- Create a recreation-oriented community.
- Develop a friendly edge by eliminating large fences along the streets.
- Establish neighborhood greens within a two-block walking distance of each home.
- Plan small housing parcels.
- Provide a variety of upscale housing opportunity.
- Develop a unique community character through architecture, landscape, and street furniture.
- Maximize the open-space edge.

Connecting the two parcels of land was accomplished by the design of a collector boulevard that links major perimeter roads to the center of the site. The clubhouse is located on a central highpoint, dedicating one of the best views on the site to the public. The golf course is routed along portions of the main boulevard and touches the adjacent roads near the main community entries (Figure 5.18). With golf-playing along the boulevard and at the entry, the image of golf extends throughout the community. Many of the golf holes are aligned east-west to maximize views across golf to the mountains.

The golf course serves to divide development parcels into smaller sizes, creating more intimate neighborhoods within the community. The development parcels exhibit a variety of housing types and price ranges, which creates diversity in the community. The existing trees, ponds, and wetlands are integrated into the golf course and often serve as a buffer area between golf and homes. This design makes playing the golf course even more exciting and protects adjacent homes from errant golf balls. These natural areas are also a pleasing contrast to the manicured look of the course.

Credit: Courtesy of DTJ Design.

Figure 5.18 The main entry at Legacy Ridge.

Community recreation centers adjacent to the collector boulevard announce each entry. These recreation centers bring the open space to the main entries, which alleviates the perception of density and suggests that Legacy Ridge is a family-oriented community. Existing large trees have been incorporated into the design of each recreation center to give the appearance that the center has been established for some time. Each cluster of homes was expected to pay a prorated share of the recreation center at the time of development, which reduced the land developer's obligation for up-front improvements. In addition to the golf clubhouse, the recreation centers are main gathering places for the community. As part of the original zoning approval, each cluster also had to create a neighborhood gathering place. These gathering places are typically small shade structures; however, in some cases, they are a more elaborate picnic structure that also houses a neighborhood mail center.

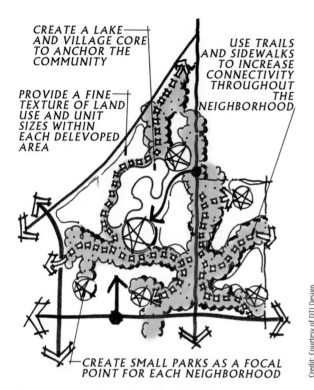

CREATE A LAKE AND VILLAGE CORE TO ANCHOR THE COMMUNITY

PROVIDE A FINE TEXTURE OF LAND USE AND UNIT SIZES WITHIN EACH DELEVOPED AREA

USE TRAILS AND SIDEWALKS TO INCREASE CONNECTIVITY THROUGHOUT THE NEIGHBORHOOD

CREATE SMALL PARKS AS A FOCAL POINT FOR EACH NEIGHBORHOOD

Figure 5.19 A traditional neighborhood-development concept idea.

Traditional Neighborhood Development (TND)
Traditional neighborhood development (TND) refers to a development pattern and detail that is an updated version of early twentieth-century small towns (see "The Ahwahnee Principles" sidebar). Central to the TND concept is the notion of an eclectic mix of housing and commercial uses grouped according to scale and massing instead of land use. Physical details include an emphasis on the quality of the street as expressed through tree lawns, garages to the rear of the lot (either garage-back or alley accessed), distinctive four-sided architecture, and civic infrastructure.

Connectivity of roads and pedestrian ways is emphasized, to disperse traffic throughout the community. The focus is more on the pedestrian realm than the vehicular realm (Figure 5.19). This community design strategy appeals to a specific market segment that must be considered when determining the most appropriate design approach.

Traditional neighborhood development grew from the public's disenchantment with the nature of poorly designed, single-use subdivisions. When the idea of community takes a back seat to yield and price, typical subdivision layout produces a sterile living environment. Streets exhibit little visual interest; vehicles travel too fast, making the street unsafe for pedestrians; houses tend to be a similar color and begin to look the same; and there is little open space to provide visual relief. In short, there is too much of the same thing. TNDs attempt to bring back the memory of quieter times and small-town living.

In an attempt to re-create the look and feel of older, denser neighborhoods as they may have evolved over time, many TNDs rely on prescriptive development and architectural standards. These standards are often written into a code that controls everything from lot access to window design. Development plans often place open space in public spaces along the street instead of in the backyards where theoretically fewer people can enjoy it. Open spaces along the street are considered safer play spaces because there are more "eyes on the space." In addition, open spaces along the street increase visual diversity and reduce the perception of higher density.

Many TNDs rely on an interconnected grid pattern to disperse traffic and create the feel of an older town. The community designer must resist the temptation to simply grid out the site; a strict grid pattern relies primarily on the building architecture to create neighborhood variety and ignores the opportunity for street design to add to community character. The plan should respond to topography and natural features that can relieve the regularity of the grid. Street lengths should be short, with visual relief at key locations. A blocked grid, on which not all of the streets go through, can also be effective in creating visual diversity (Figure 5.20). Offsetting the grid at a slight angle to major roadways is another technique to increase the visual interest. Small "found" spaces result from the intersection of the two

angles, which can be incorporated into front yards or small islands at street corners. These landscaped spaces can become little jewels along the road.

One criticism of TND is its relatively higher up-front development costs (due to slightly more infrastructure as a result of alleys, and the need to establish a strong visual presence along the street), and higher maintenance costs due to a greater amount of public space. The investment in these spaces, however, pays dividends over the life of the project by creating desirable places to live. Additionally, the increased costs should be balanced with an increase in density, to amortize the fixed costs over a greater number of units. The commu-

Credit: Courtesy of DTJ Design.

Figure 5.20 A "blocked grid" mitigates the perception of too much of the same thing.

nity builder must communicate the reality of these costs to the municipality as a means to justify greater densities.

Diversity of housing and a mix of home types are signature characteristics of TND. Larger buildings anchor key intersections, while a mix of smaller buildings defines quiet residential streets. These large buildings may be a big single-family home or a small multifamily building of condominiums or apartments. These buildings are often built with masonry and can be two and three stories high. The smaller buildings are often single-family homes or twin homes built on a variety of lot sizes. Lots may range from 35 feet wide to 70 feet wide. The smaller lots are typically alley loaded, while wider lots may be either garage-back, front loaded, or alley loaded. Front- or rear-loaded townhomes and denser row homes are home types that are also found in many TND communities.

Common to many TNDs is a small commercial core that defines a village center. The intent is to provide an alternative to driving to purchase common household items (the village core should be easy to walk to), and to create a community gathering place. In conjunction with public spaces and civic buildings, commercial uses can be very effective in creating a perceived heart of the community.

Because many commercial uses are not economically viable until the surrounding homes are built, it is important to keep the commercial buildings relatively small and to anticipate higher turnover or transitional uses until there are enough people to support the commercial uses. Locating the village commercial center closer to a major road (for increased traffic counts), or subsidizing the commercial uses for a period of time, might be necessary.

Properly designed, a village core can become a destination for adjacent neighborhoods as well, increasing the potential for economic success. Ideally, to respond to changing market conditions, obtaining approvals that allow for a variety of uses within the village core is best.

Because many commercial uses are not economically viable until the surrounding homes are built, it is important to keep the commercial buildings relatively small and to anticipate higher turnover or transitional uses until there are enough people to support the commercial uses. Locating the village commercial center closer to a major road (for increased traffic counts), or subsidizing the commercial uses for a period of time, might be necessary.

THE VILLAGE AT AUTUMN LAKE

Madison, Wisconsin

The unique characteristics of The Village at Autumn Lake site were immediately apparent during the initial site analysis. The 280-acre site is strategically located on the near east side of Madison, close to the East Towne Mall (major shopping area) and the town of Sun Prairie, home to American Family Insurance (major employment). Although close to both shopping and employment, the site had the appearance of being isolated because of a major highway, a rail line, and a steep, wooded slope. This isolation suggested that a small village could be created and not feel like it was an extension of a typical suburban subdivision. The site is part of the headwaters area for Starkweather Creek. As was previously mentioned, the concept of a lake village became the underlying theme for the vision created for The Village at Autumn Lake.

The community is organized around the lake as the primary community amenity. Nothing speaks to the image of a small southern Wisconsin village like life around a lake. Water activities are central to Wisconsin life. Depending on the season, fishing, sailing, swimming, boating, water skiing, and ice skating are all activities residents regularly enjoy. As the visual center of the community, the lake creates accessible open space and enhances the value of all the homes within the village. Manicured parks along the shore are places for family gatherings and picnics. Fireworks over the lake are a valued Wisconsin tradition that can be continued at The Village at Autumn Lake.

Adjacent to the lake is the community school and a 6-acre community park. Smaller neighborhood parks, ranging in size from .2 acres to 3 acres, are focal points within each of the five surrounding neighborhoods. These parks respond to the needs of the residents: A park serving a young family's starter-home neighborhood has playgrounds and open play fields, while the park serving active retirees has walking trails, flower beds, and benches. Each home is within a three-minute walk from at least one neighborhood park. The Midland Green, in the center of the village core, is a place for more formal gatherings. The farmer's market and other community-wide events can take place at The Midland Green, which is across the street from a public plaza near the lake (Figure 5.21).

All of the parks are linked by an extensive sidewalk and trail system that winds throughout the community. Regionally, the site connects to the bikeway running parallel to the rail line. This link will eventually connect to downtown Madison. From this trail are three connections into the site. One trail connects directly to the Autumn Lake Trail, a 1.0-mile loop around the lake. This trail is a combination of a soft, natural trail, a boardwalk through the wetland area on the north end of the lake, and a paved trail adjacent to the village core. At the southern end of the lake, the Autumn Lake Trail connects to the Ravines Trail near the village core. This 1.2-mile trail connects the community east-west across Felland Road (the major north-south road) and terminates in a neighborhood recreation center on the eastern part of the site. Near Felland Road, the Ravines Trail links to a small 0.2-mile trail, the Pine Loop, which runs along the base of the slope through the pine trees to Pines Park. A 0.4-mile Woodland Trail connects the east side of Felland Road north-south to the Ravines Trail. Together, these trails provide pedestrian and bikeway access throughout the community and support the notion of a people-friendly place.

The natural environment is a central focus of the village. The plan creates and enhances many environmental features. A variety of lake depths and edge treatments results in a wide range of both aquatic and terrestrial habitats. Fish, amphibians, small mammals, and birds will find food and shelter in and around the lake. The lake's water quality is protected by leading-edge design concepts, including bioswales to filter and clean water prior to entering the lake, and aeration systems to ensure high dissolved-oxygen content. Water gardens and groundwater-recharge areas around the existing wetlands enhance the viability of Starkweather Creek. At the upper end of The Ravines and along wooded slopes, man-made impacts will be minimized. Soft trails will be fit into the hillside to minimize cut and fill and tree removal, and a large portion of the wooded areas will be left intact to provide habitat for birds and larger mammals.

At Autumn Lake, the quality of the street is important to the look and feel of the community. The width of pavement and parkways, and the parking bays, tree lawns, and setbacks are balanced to the type of street and the amount of traffic. Small, residential streets are narrow, with smaller tree lawns and reduced setbacks. The compressed spaces slow traffic down, which

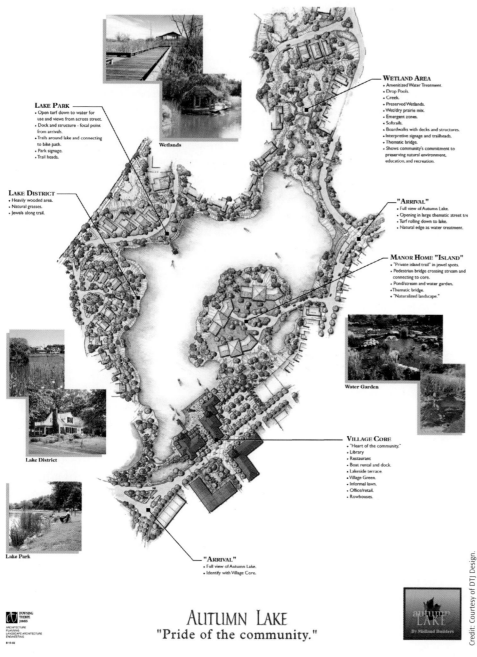

LAKE PARK
- Open turf down to water for use and views from across street.
- Dock and structure - focal point from arrivals.
- Trails around lake and connecting to bike path.
- Park signage.
- Trail heads.

Wetlands

WETLAND AREA
- Amenitized Water Treatment.
- Drop Pools.
- Creek.
- Preserved Wetlands.
- Wet/dry prairie mix.
- Emergent zones.
- Softrails.
- Boardwalks with decks and structures.
- Interpretive signage and trailheads.
- Thematic bridge.
- Shows community's commitment to preserving natural environment, education, and recreation.

LAKE DISTRICT
- Heavily wooded area.
- Natural grasses.
- Jewels along trail.

"ARRIVAL"
- Full view of Autumn Lake.
- Opening in large thematic street tre
- Turf rolling down to lake.
- Natural edge as water treatment.

MANOR HOME "ISLAND"
- "Private island trail" in jewel spots.
- Pedestrian bridge crossing stream and connecting to core.
- Pond/stream and water garden.
- Thematic bridge.
- "Naturalized landscape."

Water Garden

Lake District

VILLAGE CORE
- "Heart of the community."
- Library
- Restaurant
- Boat rental and dock.
- Lakeside terrace.
- Village Green.
- Informal lawn.
- Office/retail.
- Rowhouses.

Lake Park

"ARRIVAL"
- Full view of Autumn Lake.
- Identify with Village Core.

DUNNING THORPE JAMES
ARCHITECTURE
PLANNING
LANDSCAPE ARCHITECTURE
ENGINEERING
8-13-02

AUTUMN LAKE
"Pride of the community."

autumn LAKE
By Midland Builders

Figure 5.21 The village core becomes a place for community events to happen.

makes the streets safer for pedestrians. The entry boulevards celebrate the arrival into Autumn Lake with landscaped medians and views to the lake. At the village core, the street transforms into a more urban street edge, with wide sidewalks for possible sitting at the neighborhood café or other similar use.

In an effort to obtain alternate street standards, a study of some of the most charming neighborhoods in Madison was completed. To garner support for the study, the mayor and the community development director identified these neighborhoods. Extensive photographs and physical measurement were taken in the neighborhoods, to quantify the quality of the spaces. Road widths, tree lawns, sidewalks, and setbacks were all measured and recorded. Homes were photographed and analyzed with respect to form, massing, and detail. Open spaces were also measured and evaluated.

The result was a summary book that guided the creation of the standards for The Village at Autumn Lake (Figure 5.22). A precedent existed in the city and was proclaimed by key individuals to be very desirable. Autumn Lake is simply trying to emulate these charming neighborhoods. The different street standards and setbacks are written into the PUD for Autumn Lake and have been endorsed by the director of community development.

There are 12 different housing types within the 1,102 units, from lake-front cottages to manor homes at 40 du/ac, located on the island in the lake. Homes have either front-loaded, garage-back, or alley-loaded garages to mitigate the negative impact of garages on the quality of the street. The overall density is relatively high (3.9 du/ac gross and 7.6 du/ac net), to allow the developer to pay for the significant investment in community open space and features. The commercial area is planned for 45,000 square feet of use, including a destination restaurant on the lake and the builder's design center for all of its Madison communities. Homes are designed with a simple Midwest-farmhouse architectural flavor, using brick and wood, with front porches and steep pitched roofs.

Blended Community Design

Blended community design utilizes characteristics from both TND and open-space community design to form a hybrid (Figure 5.23). Streets are less formal than a TND, they respond more to open spaces and other natural features, and they may have more dead-ends or cul-de-sacs. Housing types are not mixed as much as they might be in a TND, they show up in smaller blocks of the same land use instead of being mixed on a lot-by-lot basis, and there is generally a more even split between front-loaded and rear-loaded homes.

Although not completely true to either design strategy, a blended-community design approach offers benefits. Important among those benefits is a greater acceptance by municipalities that have not yet embraced the narrower street standards and reduced setbacks of the TND. Without different standards for streets, the amount of additional land required for wide streets, large setbacks, and alleys can make a TND approach economically infeasible. Additionally, these same municipalities also may not understand the tradeoffs between increased density and the community builder's ability to provide civic amenities. As a result, the community builder must often provide more natural open-space amenities for the community.

Another benefit of a blended-community design strategy is a simplified marketing

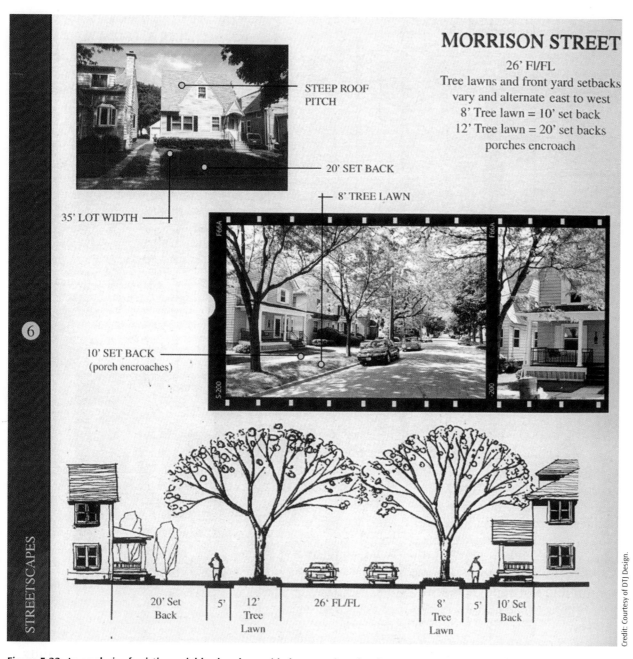

MORRISON STREET

26' Fl/FL
Tree lawns and front yard setbacks
vary and alternate east to west
8' Tree lawn = 10' set back
12' Tree lawn = 20' set backs
porches encroach

STEEP ROOF PITCH

20' SET BACK

8' TREE LAWN

35' LOT WIDTH

10' SET BACK
(porch encroaches)

20' Set Back   5'   12' Tree Lawn   26' FL/FL   8' Tree Lawn   5'   10' Set Back

Credit: Courtesy of DTJ Design.

STREETSCAPES

6

Figure 5.22 An analysis of existing neighborhoods provided appropriate development standards for The Village at Autumn Lake.

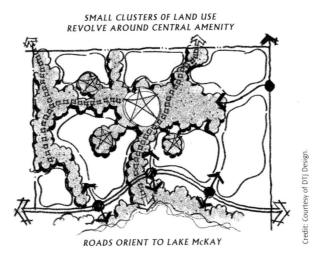

SMALL CLUSTERS OF LAND USE
REVOLVE AROUND CENTRAL AMENITY

ROADS ORIENT TO LAKE McKAY

Figure 5.23 A blended-community concept idea.

Credit: Courtesy of DTJ Design.

Visual diversity within a blended community is enhanced in that noncompeting builders can build distinctly different housing types in close proximity to each other. Diversity must be expressed in both housing design and price. This diversity creates a more pleasing street scene and expands the potential market for the community, which in turn can make the community more competitive in the regional marketplace and can speed absorption. Fast absorption indicates a highly desirable community, which can cause rapid appreciation in home prices for new buyers and for the builder. Faster absorption can also accelerate the building of amenities, which makes the community even more desirable.

approach. The wide variety of housing types, and the scattered location of those housing types in a TND, can make marketing by more than one builder difficult. Each builder would have to participate in a community marketing center that describes the community story, and rely on a greeter to prequalify buyers and direct them to the most appropriate housing type. Many builders are wary of this type of cross-marketing, believing that they will miss an opportunity to sell buyers on their homes. In a blended community, however, each builder can agree to build all of the same home type in a small parcel and create a sales center within that parcel for that housing product. Builders can individually communicate the community story and demonstrate their houses to prospective buyers (Figure 5.24). In this way, the individual builder has more control over how much money and effort he or she puts into establishing the community image and marketing to buyers.

Credit: Courtesy of DTJ Design.

Figure 5.24 Specially designed sculpture can help tell the community story.

MCKAY LANDING

Broomfield, Colorado

As a typical suburban municipality, Broomfield historically had approved subdivisions with large lots, wide streets, and generous setbacks. Homes were usually detached single-family or apartments, developed in large tracts of the same lot size or building design. With the rapid growth of the late 1990s, the city administration felt that the historical development pattern was contributing to sprawl and needed to change. After some investigation of TND, the city was interested in exploring a strategy that had elements of a TND and that kept many of its existing development standards. As a relatively conservative community, Broomfield was reluctant to make a complete change in its development standards, preferring instead to allow a developer to create an overall project theme and seek variances as necessary to implement the theme. This uncertainty demanded that the developer look to a blended-community design strategy to minimize risk as the development went ahead.

To create the diversity that the approach suggests, the original developer formed a *limited-liability corporation (LLC)* with another builder. Together, they shared in the expense of creating the common amenities, and each developed and marketed an exclusive house type within the community. All of the housing types were designed with similar architectural inspiration that provided a visual continuity through a western waterfront theme.

The results of this design approach have been very successful for both the city of Broomfield and the community builder. As you drive into the community from the south, the view changes from sixplex townhomes, to open space, to rear-loaded patio homes, to front- and rear-loaded townhomes, to move-up single-family homes, all within a few short blocks. A trip around McKay Park Circle in the center of the site reveals front- and rear-loaded townhomes and move-up single-family, luxury single-family, conventional single-family, and rear-loaded patio homes (Figure 5.25). This visual diversity has been an appealing feature of McKay Landing. The central open space, which consists of a community center with a pool, day care, and deli; a one-acre tot lot; a large park with ball fields (Figure 5.26); and a neighborhood school, is well appreciated by the residents. And it is paid for by a higher overall density for McKay Landing than that of neighboring developments. One builder reported obtaining approximately 5 percent more per unit for the same house at McKay Landing than one that was available in another development just four miles away. This price differential is evidence that buyers appreciate, and will pay for, community design.

The street pattern at McKay Landing varies depending on which housing type is being built. In the rear-loaded patio homes, the streets take on a blocked, grid approach, with small parks and islands in the alley breaking up the formality of the grid. Streets terminate at open spaces and the community center. In the luxury single-family area, the street is a narrow, winding boulevard with oversized, landscaped cul-de-sacs terminating the views. Each cluster of homes has a special landscaped feature in front. In the move-up single-family homes, the streets respond more to open spaces with small parks and cul-de-sacs. In the sixplex townhome parcel, the street design allows a small, central park to be the focal point and offers views to the building architecture instead of garage doors (Figure 5.27).

Detached sidewalks, open-space trails, and roads connect McKay Landing to the larger community. A paved regional trail extends along the creek to the south, while a soft trail connects the park adjacent to McKay Lake to the central community park in McKay Landing. Smaller trails connect the park in the luxury-home parcel to a neighboring park in the adjacent development, and various small parks in the community to the recreation center. Benches and trash receptacles identify resting places along the trail and encourage users to appreciate the beauty of the site.

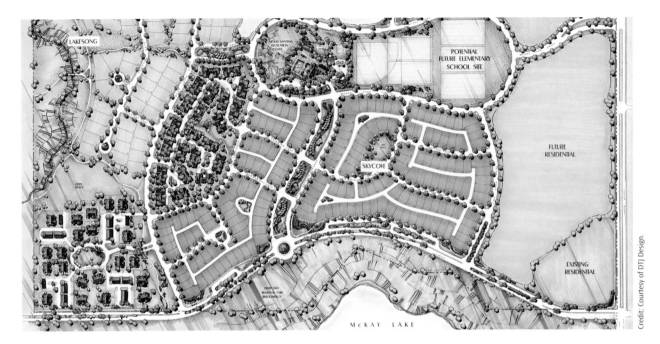

Credit: Courtesy of DTJ Design.

Figure 5.25 A variety of home styles blended together creates visual diversity within McKay Landing.

Credit: Courtesy of DTJ Design.

Figure 5.26 The community center at McKay Landing includes a pool, community building, day care, and deli.

Figure 5.27 A small gathering place should be designed to serve a small cluster of homes.

Mixed-Use Community Design

For the purposes of this book, *mixed-use communities* differ from those offered in TND by increased intensity of uses and fewer natural open spaces. In a suburban setting, mixed-use community development usually takes the form of low- to mid-rise buildings two, three, or four stories high. The mixed-use community might be the core area of a larger, suburban community (Figure 5.28). Retail or office uses may occupy the ground floor, with residential units above. Live/work spaces, in which the ground level is an office or shop and the living portion of the unit is above, are also an appropriate solution to mixing uses. Larger shops, such as a deli or specialty grocery, may anchor a building. Ideally, uses should connect across property boundaries to provide a seamless transition between developments. Street patterns may be looser, with small, manicured

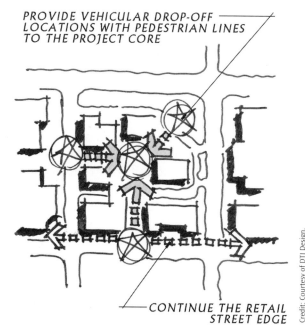

PROVIDE VEHICULAR DROP-OFF LOCATIONS WITH PEDESTRIAN LINES TO THE PROJECT CORE

CONTINUE THE RETAIL STREET EDGE

Credit: Courtesy of DTJ Design.

Figure 5.28 A mixed-use community concept idea.

open spaces providing visual relief to the higher density of uses. Street edges are well-landscaped, with wide, detached sidewalks connecting neighborhood open spaces. Street trees provide shade and visual relief.

In a more urban setting, mixed-use development responds to higher land prices by increasing residential and commercial densities. Uses may be blended vertically, as in residential over retail or office, or horizontally, where each building is a separate use linked by public spaces. Floor-area ratios can exceed .5:1, thus requiring structured parking. Open spaces are usually limited to urban plazas or a community green.

The quality of the architecture and how it relates to the street and pedestrians is a focus of mixed-use community design. Architectural rhythms and building bays defined by windows and doors should relate to human-scale dimensions at the street, as opposed to a suburban, auto-oriented scale. Large buildings should step back horizontally as they rise vertically, to create a human scale along the street. Retail or office uses should embrace the street, with windows and doors bringing life to the ground level. Where possible, uses should spill out onto the sidewalk to create a connection between the inside and outside of the building. This connection can increase community life in key places. Highly tactile materials such as brick or stone can enhance the visual quality of the building and create a finer texture along the street.

A mixed-use community should reflect the community fabric around it. It should complement vehicular and pedestrian connections across the site, and building massing should respect the neighbors and views. Building massing may visually anchor a key intersection and transition to lower-level buildings adjacent to neighboring residential areas. Major pedestrian linkages should be continued through the site and incorporated into the use and design. Pedestrian plazas should welcome people from the street and provide a place for community events. The plaza becomes a place for concerts and festivals that bring life to the community. Water can be introduced to provide playful movement, and quiet sitting areas protected by trees and shrubs can be provided for contemplation or reading.

Urban Infill

As a community-design strategy, urban infill has many unique characteristics. The style and intensity of the community must respond to existing uses adjacent to the site. If it is too large, the community can overwhelm its neighbors; if it is too small, the community can seem lost and insignificant. Every effort must be made to work with the neighbors on design, massing, and intensity to facilitate project approvals. At the very least, the neighbors must remain neutral during the approval process, or the project will face costly delays.

It is necessary to work within the limitations of existing infrastructure, including water, sewer, and surrounding roads. Completing extensive off-site improvements in a built environment is difficult and expensive. Potential disruption to existing services tends to bring out the worst in people who can stop, or delay, the community. Invariably, additional construction costs must be considered when one builds an infill community.

Because parking is at a premium in urban locations, the site should be serviced by alter-

KIERLAND COMMONS

Phoenix, Arizona

Kierland Commons is a large, mixed-use development in Phoenix. To the south, the elevations of Camelback and Squaw Peak mountains are visible in the distance; to the north, the Tonto National Forest provides a striking visual backdrop. In the foreground, the Kierland golf course is northwest of the site, with the Westin resort directly to the west. Existing two- and four-story office and retail buildings create a hard edge along the Greenway Parkway. Retail along Main Street defines adjacent uses east and west, while multifamily and retail define uses across Kierland Boulevard to the north. The following concept study, comprising residential lofts over retail, *mid-rise residential*, and urban row homes, illustrates one potential development scenario for a portion of the site (Figure 5.29).

To encourage a stronger retail experience that would provide a continuity of retail use along Main Street was a high priority. Other design goals included maximizing the buildings and orientation for views, creating a sense of arrival and identity, a strong sense of place and home, and a secure and safe environment for shoppers and residents. The development program called for 140 residential units and 30,000 square feet of retail uses. The new buildings were replacing surface parking for adjacent office uses, so an additional 574 parking spaces were also required.

To meet the design goals, secure and segregated parking for shoppers, office users, and residents was proposed under each building. Various parking floors would provide secure access to residential units through segregated elevators. Separate automobile drop-offs for each residential building type would create a sense of individuality within the project. A series of exterior gardens, courtyard spaces, and water features would create a distinction between public and private spaces and provide visual relief to the urban environment. A continuous pedestrian space would connect each of the primary buildings in the block. An on-site fitness center and business center would complete the amenities for the community. The mid-rise residential building would step back from the street, and all of the architecture would complement the existing architecture of Kierland Commons (Figures 5.30).

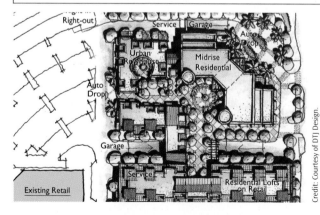

Credit: Courtesy of DTJ Design.

Credit: Courtesy of DTJ Design.

Figure 5.29 The concept plan for a portion of Kierland Commons continues the existing urban fabric.

Figure 5.30 Building massing steps back on upper floors.

native transportation options. These might include light rail, commuter trains, bus systems, and walkways and trails. Many of the community amenities must come from the surrounding, existing community infrastructure and meet the needs of the buyers. Shopping, plays and concerts, art museums, and libraries are a few of the amenities found in urban areas. Existing community parks and open spaces should be close enough to also act as amenities for the site.

ONE BOULDER PLAZA

Boulder, Colorado

When One Boulder Plaza was originally conceived as an urban infill, mixed-use community, the site was occupied by an outdated office building and parking. With its location one block from the Pearl Street Mall in downtown Boulder and across Canyon Boulevard from Boulder Creek, the site has terrific views of the Flatirons, a striking geologic formation in the foothills adjacent to Boulder (Figure 5.31). Demand for residential uses in downtown Boulder is high, and the city boasts an active nightlife. Community facilities and an active lifestyle are trademarks of this university town.

The design for One Boulder Plaza includes four buildings facing each other across 13th Street. Between the buildings is a year-round plaza with a winter skating rink and a bikeway separated from traffic by a landscape median that links the Pearl Street Mall to Central Park and the Boulder Creek bike path (Figure 5.32). The first building includes 67,000 square feet of residential uses in 32 separate condominium units, and 116,000 square feet of office, including a new bank with five drive-through lanes and 354 parking spaces. The residential condominiums are located on the second, third, and fourth floors, and the units have terrific views of the Flatirons to the southwest or downtown Boulder to the north. In 2002, the market-rate units sold for approximately $500 per square foot, some of the highest values in the metro-Denver area.

A bank, a restaurant, and retail uses comprise the first floor of both buildings, and large glass areas allow pedestrians to see into the buildings. A wide sidewalk along Canyon Boulevard creates a safe place along the busy traffic lanes. The building architecture incorporates tower elements on the corners and brick banding to break up the massing. Terraces provide outdoor living spaces for residential units and detail on the building façade (Figure 5.33). Residents can enjoy the twice-weekly farmer's market located adjacent to the site on 13th Street. One Boulder Plaza meshes well with the vibrant, active lifestyle of downtown Boulder.

Figure 5.31 The Flatirons provide a unique amenity for One Boulder Plaza homes and offices.

Figure 5.33 Building architecture can enhance the quality of the street.

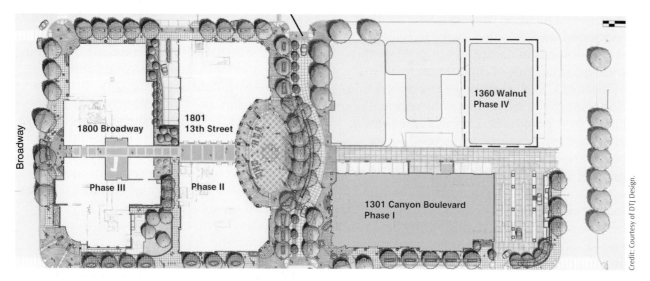

Broadway

1800 Broadway

Phase III

1801 13th Street

Phase II

1360 Walnut Phase IV

1301 Canyon Boulevard Phase I

Figure 5.32 The site plan brings four buildings together around a central gathering place.

The Community Designer

Balancing the competing interests of the site, the market, and money within the context of a strong community story requires unique individuals. Unlike engineering, quality community design has no hard and fast rules. Each design solution must be matched perfectly to the specific situation. Community designers must evaluate a myriad of options at once to determine the best course of action. They must understand the natural environment and the built environment. Intense, logical thinking must be tempered by an affinity for people and an eye for the aesthetic.

Few professions teach the full complement of skills necessary to become a quality community designer. Some of the skills are intuitive, developed over many years of careful observation of the built environment. It is important to look not just at what is there, but also at how people react to, or interact with, the spaces. The community designer must learn to identify the qualities of spaces, how are they composed, and how they evoke feelings. Other skills are social in nature, developed by exposure to a multitude of experiences in a variety of locations. Such skills make any design solution less provincial, untainted by regional prejudices or expectations. Experience designing, and experience evaluating the results over several years, are absolutely vital to the development of a quality community designer.

Of the physical design professions, architecture and landscape architecture provide the best basic education for community designers—architecture because architects develop an understanding of the vertical elements of community, and landscape architecture because of landscape architects' in-depth knowledge of environmental and man-made systems. More landscape architects tend to become community designers through their interest in larger spaces, while architects often focus on individual buildings and their context. Landscape architects can enhance their abilities as community designers by learning more about vertical architecture and human behavior. Architects need to supplement their education by learning more about the environment and man-made systems.

Managing the Community Design Team

When evaluating community-design experience, judging how successful a community designer has been in creating a sense of place is more important than simply judging how many communities or neighborhoods someone has completed. Laying out subdivisions is not necessarily effective community-design experience. It is important to study the work, both in the plans and supporting documents and in the actual built environment. The community builder should visit communities designed by potential consultants.

One hallmark of an experienced community designer is that he or she provides creative solutions to difficult issues. The community designer should be able to discuss the community story, how the design responds to site opportunities and constraints, and what issues influenced the final community design. Often, current development standards do not facilitate creative site design at higher densities. New standards, or variations to existing standards, are necessary to create housing solutions that appeal to the market. An experienced community designer can help achieve support for appropriate standards.

Being able to articulate a vision is another characteristic of an experienced community designer. Designers can do this through photographs, sketches, models, and even words. The power of the vision is greatest in combination. A skillfully conceived and communicated vision will increase public acceptance of the community. Community builders should look carefully to see whether they can understand the visions their consultants have developed.

The Design Team

The community designer is only one member of the design team. Creative input and dialogue from all members of the team add to the potential for success. Engineers can bring creative solutions to engineering issues. They can bring the latest technology and best practices, for example, to resolve drainage and stormwater concerns. Each profession brings a different perspective that adds to the quality of the solution. Marketing consultants or salespeople can communicate the long-term value of the community. Every building or lot that is sold should support the vision in some way. When the vision is implemented successfully, values for the builder and the buyer continue to escalate.

Communication skills and accepting responsibility are key traits of an effective community-design team. All consultants should clearly know what is expected of them. The team leader has the responsibility to ensure that each member is kept up-to-date and informed of decisions. Group e-mail lists and job meeting reports that present information on what is discussed, and who is responsible for what tasks, help the team stay focused. Team members should establish a schedule for their work, and then, barring unforeseen circumstances, be held accountable to the schedule. The team's collective expertise results in better project execution from start to finish.

As with most things, it is reasonable to expect to pay more for quality. What is also reasonable is to expect that the additional cost is less than the added benefit from the work. Quality community design should pay for itself many times over through higher prices, faster sales, and increasing appreciation. Interestingly, builders and developers often pay 3 percent to 7 percent sales commissions for homes that, when well-designed, are easier to sell. Accordingly, it is reasonable to invest .75 percent to 1 percent of the sales price for community design services that create the value to be sold. "Chapter 7: Financing" discusses what the community builder should budget for the design and construction of community elements, and what to expect for a return on investment.

The Ahwahnee Principles

In 1991 a group of urban-design professionals met to create guiding principles for new town development. These professionals included Andres Duany, Elizabeth Plater-Zyberk, Michael Corbett, Stefanos Polyzoides, Elizabeth Moule, Peter Calthorpe, and Peter Katz. These principles are the philosophical basis for *New Urbanism*. Although some may argue against specific recommendations, for the most part, these principles are accepted nationwide. They are reprinted in their entirety below.

Preamble

Existing patterns of urban and suburban development seriously impair our quality of life. The symptoms are: more congestion and air pollution resulting from our increased dependence on automobiles, the loss of precious open space, the need for costly improvements to roads and public services, the inequitable distribution of economic resources, and the loss of a sense of community. By drawing upon the best from the past and present, we can plan communities that will more successfully serve the needs of those who live and work within them. Such planning should adhere to certain fundamental principles.

Community Principles

1. All planning should be in the form of complete and integrated communities containing housing, shops, work places, schools, parks, and civic facilities essential to the daily life of the residents.
2. Community size should be designed so that housing, jobs, daily needs, and other activities are within easy walking distance of each other.
3. As many activities as possible should be located within easy walking distance of transit stops.
4. A community should contain a diversity of housing types to enable citizens from a wide range of economic levels and age groups to live within its boundaries.
5. Businesses within the community should provide a range of job types for the community's residents.
6. The location and character of the community should be consistent with a larger transit network.
7. The community should have a center focus that combines commercial, civic, cultural, and recreational uses.
8. The community should contain an ample supply of specialized open space in the form of squares, greens, and parks whose frequent use is encouraged through placement and design.
9. Public spaces should be designed to encourage the attention and presence of people at all hours of the day and night.
10. Each community or cluster of communities should have a well-defined edge, such as agricultural greenbelts or wildlife corridors, permanently protected from development.
11. Streets, pedestrian paths, and bike paths should contribute to a system of fully-connected and interesting routes to all destinations. Their design should encourage pedestrian and bicycle use by being small and spatially defined by buildings, trees, and lighting, and by discouraging high-speed traffic.
12. Wherever possible, the natural terrain, drainage, and vegetation of the community should be preserved, with superior examples contained within parks and greenbelts.
13. The community design should help conserve resources and minimize waste.
14. Communities should provide for the efficient use of water through the use of natural drainage, drought tolerant landscaping, and recycling.
15. The street orientation, the placement of buildings, and the use of shading should contribute to the energy efficiency of the community.

Regional Principles

1. The regional land-use planning structure should be integrated within a larger transportation network built around transit rather than freeways.
2. Regions should be bounded by and provide a continuous system of greenbelt/wildlife corridors to be determined by natural conditions.
3. Regional institutions and services (government, stadiums, museums, etc.) should be located in the urban core.
4. Materials and methods of constructions should be specific to the region, exhibiting a continuity of history and culture and compatibility with the climate, to

encourage the development of local character and community identity.

Implementation Principles

1. The general plan should be updated to incorporate the above principles
2. Rather than allowing developer-initiated, piecemeal development, local governments should take charge of the planning process. General plans should designate where new growth, infill, or redevelopment will be allowed to occur.
3. Prior to any development, a specific plan should be prepared based on these principles.
4. Plans should be developed through an open process, and participants in the process should be provided visual models of all planning proposals.

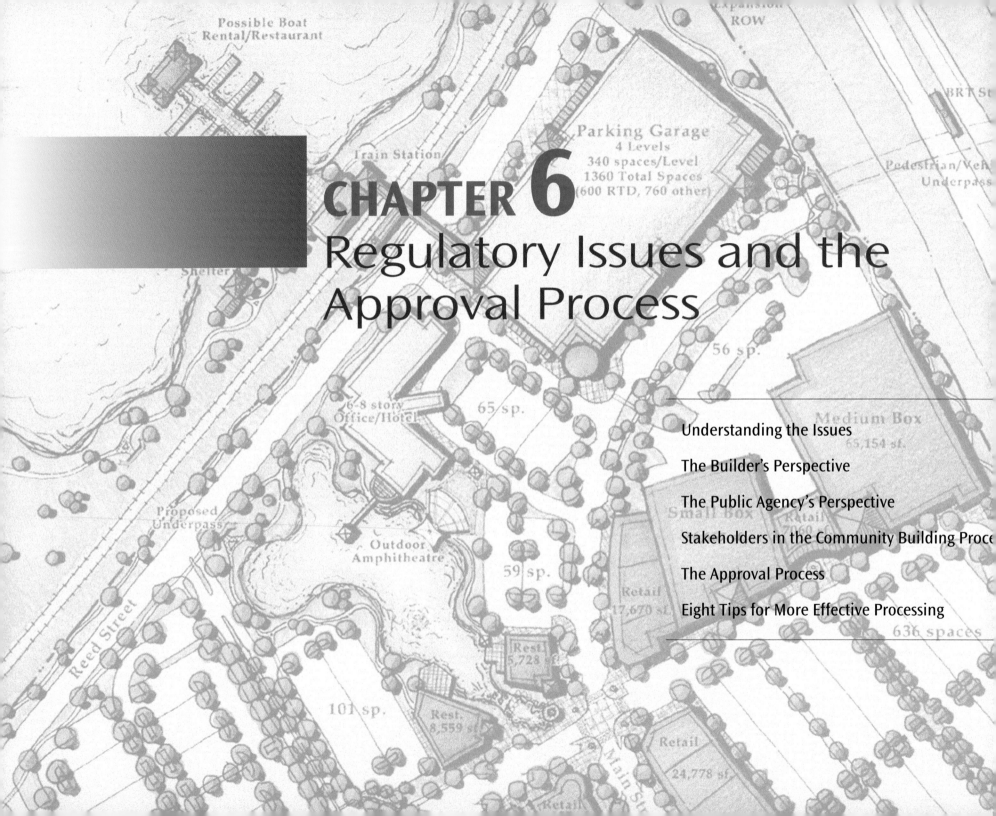

CHAPTER 6
Regulatory Issues and the Approval Process

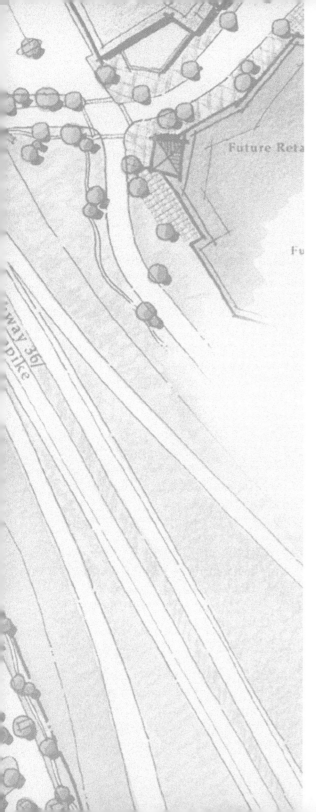

Regulatory issues are affecting community design now more than ever. The very best community design is wasted if the community can't be approved and built. From antiquated regulations to virulent no-growth attitudes, the public-approval process is increasingly time consuming and expensive. Understanding these unresolved issues guides an appropriate strategy to succeed with project approvals. This chapter identifies, from both the builder's perspective and the public agency's perspective, some of the issues that are common across the United States. Resolving these issues overcomes barriers to quality community design and builds trust between the building industry and the public. All stakeholders must stay open to new ideas and approaches that will resolve these issues. This chapter also identifies the stakeholders who are active in the approval process, presents a process that has been proven effective in resolving many of the issues, and makes suggestions to reduce conflict.

Understanding the Issues

To adequately address the regulatory issues, it is necessary to take a hard look at them from the perspective of the primary stakeholders. From the builder's perspective, regulatory issues that act as potential barriers to great community design include the design-review process, outdated regulations and standards, the training and talents of municipal staff, the politics of growth, a perceived desire on the part of municipal government to shift the burden of solving many of society's problems to the builder, the qualifications of municipal boards and councils, and the conflicting desires of the public. From the public's perspective, these potential issues include a lack of concern by builders for the greater community, unproven design approaches, little sensitivity for the environment, a perception of greed on the part of builders and developers, a perceived desire on the part of builders to make money at the expense of the municipality, and builders' lack of commitment to good design as evidenced by sprawling subdivisions across the country. Exposing these issues should help each stakeholder understand the other's perspective and evaluate what each can do to resolve the issues.

The Builder's Perspective

The design-review process is inherently clumsy and burdensome. Community builders can spend significant time and money developing plans, only to be mired in endless reviews over relatively insignificant issues. Even when builders include municipal staff in the early stages of the design process (as they should), there is no certainty that the project will be allowed to move forward as planned. Unknown factors, such as a small but vocal group of citizens opposing the project, a board member's pet peeve, or even a councilperson running for elected office, can derail the project or cause major delays. This lack of certainty regarding schedule and phased approvals increases the investment and risk for community builders, which subsequently increases the price of housing.

A process that encourages phased reviews, coupled with a binding commitment that the parties will live by the agreements made at those reviews, is more efficient and useful. Each phase becomes the benchmark for the next level of design and is used to guide the review. If the plans meet the design intent of the previous phase, the project should be allowed to move ahead quickly. To encourage builders and developers to enhance the design of their communities, a streamlined approval process should be provided as a reward for those who make the necessary commitments. It is not unreasonable to expect that the municipality invest the energy necessary to quickly review a project when it expects the community builder to make a similar investment in community design.

Outdated regulations and standards keep the design of communities from evolving. In many respects, the sprawl that many people find so distasteful is a product of the regulations that municipalities enforce (Figure 6.1). Municipalities have spent considerable time creating regulations and standards, so they often feel compelled to use them as long as possible. Additionally, staff can become efficient at regulating the standards, and some municipalities feel change might cause confusion. As a result, municipalities are slow to respond to different community-design approaches and people's desires about how they want their communities to look and feel.

Regulations and standards were developed for a purpose. They were designed to protect the public's health, safety, and welfare by providing access, air, water, and light to property. Many regulations are based on the premise that quantifiable engineering solutions to problems are the most effective way to promote the public good. Municipalities support this notion because of concern for liability when decisions are made on any other, less quantifiable basis. As a result, many planning commissions and city councils are resolved to weigh objective engineering and legal input more than subjective planning input.

Figure 6.1 The visual quality of the community is often dictated by existing standards.

Bringing the human side of the equation into balance with the engineering and legal side, however, is appropriate. Consideration must be given to how the community will "live." These social and aesthetic aspects of community are as important as moving cars from one place to the other or providing water and sewer service. The quality of the place is important to people's perception of where they live and how they interact with each other. When they feel a part of their community, people treat it with respect. Public agencies should establish community-design goals, and then communicate those goals to the builders, without trying to design neighborhoods and communities.

Creating more flexible, performance-based goals and standards is also appropriate. The concept of one solution fitting all situations should be substituted with an open-minded approach to create specific standards for each solution, based on function and design. This style mirrors the approach advocated by original planned-unit-development ordinances (PUDs); but PUDs often lacked the flexibility to respond to changing market conditions, and most municipalities are reluctant to allow alternative development and land-use standards. Efforts must be made to overcome this reluctance. Proven techniques from other communities can act as precedents for approval without undue scrutiny.

The training and talent of municipal planners becomes more important with a balanced approach between planning and engineering. Many municipal planning staffs are trained as policy planners and have little, or no, experience in physical design. This limitation is marginally acceptable when these personnel are required to simply implement existing standards; however, when they are charged with evaluating how a community design responds to performance-based goals, they must have a thorough working knowledge of physical design. They should also understand the fundamental realities of financing, sales and marketing, and construction, or include those municipal specialists as part of the comprehensive review team for each project. Without that context, their evaluations have little basis in reality. They do not need to know the details of the market, but they do need to know what the market desires.

Municipalities should compete with private-sector design firms to hire, and retain, the best designers they can. These designers must be trained to evaluate the built environment, with a keen eye toward concepts and details. They must constantly seek to learn and understand new approaches, and construction materials and methods. The municipalities should consider creating a research-and-development budget to allow their people to remain on par with the private sector. To the extent they choose to follow these guidelines, municipalities can improve their staff and not hire consultants.

The politics of growth is like a pendulum that swings between the need for growth and the negative consequences of growth. On the one hand, when economic times are tough, municipalities and regions adopt policies that encourage growth, to attract business to stimulate the economy. As discussed in Chapter 2, job growth invariably generates population growth and, by inference, household growth. On the other hand, as population and household growth occur, basic services such as sewer and water systems, roads, and schools are stressed as improvements struggle to keep up with demand. When these stressful changes occur, people (and, by representation, politicians) react with an outcry against growth. This cycle is divisive and completely avoidable.

The necessary action is for municipalities to proactively *prepare* for growth instead of *react* to growth. Political will is necessary to invest in the infrastructure for growth before demand outpaces the ability to keep up with growth. This position relies on the belief that there is a benefit to growth, not just a cost. Before the thought that new residents had to pay the entire cost of growth, many communities taxed themselves to create the necessary infrastructure to accommodate future growth. Much like people today who tax themselves to purchase open space for future generations, community leaders understood that, properly managed, growth was a good thing. As jobs and people moved in, the entire community benefited (Figure 6.2). Communities should evaluate the benefits of taxing themselves to provide community amenities that meet the needs of the residents.

Builders are sometimes asked to carry the burdens of our society through policies and regulations that benefit the entire community at the expense of the building industry. Mandatory affordable-housing programs and significant off-site infrastructure improvements are two common burdens builders shoulder. Mandatory affordable-housing

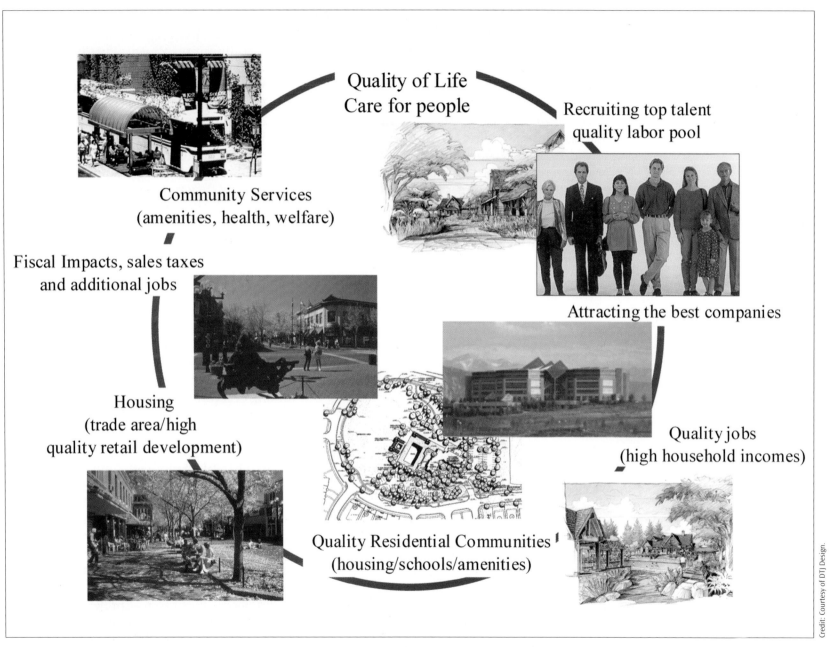

Quality of Life
Care for people

Recruiting top talent
quality labor pool

Community Services
(amenities, health, welfare)

Attracting the best companies

Fiscal Impacts, sales taxes
and additional jobs

Housing
(trade area/high
quality retail development)

Quality jobs
(high household incomes)

Quality Residential Communities
(housing/schools/amenities)

Figure 6.2 Attracting high-quality housing attracts high-quality jobs and increases tax revenue.

programs require that builders offer a percentage of their homes to low- or moderate-income buyers. These homes are usually subsidized by higher prices on market-rate units. With mandatory affordable housing, the irony is that the industries that actually create the need for affordable housing (retail, some manufacturing, services) are not asked to help subsidize that needed housing. The higher prices on the market-rate units actually contribute to higher housing prices, which intensifies the need for affordable housing. A more balanced approach is to have all industries contribute to an affordable-housing fund, wherein the municipality pays builders market rate to construct units that they sell or manage at affordable prices. More progressive industry leaders will recognize that this approach will ultimately benefit their companies because employees will be able to purchase reasonably priced housing.

Significant off-site infrastructure improvements that may require a pro-rated share of the off-site improvement are often exacted from builders. The choices are usually presented as either build the improvement and wait for future reimbursement by other landowners as the improvements develop, or do not build. In some cases, the existing infrastructure is overextended, and builder/developers are being asked to rectify an existing problem before he or she can move ahead. Municipalities are often reluctant to accept any of the financial burdens to solve existing problems when they can force the building industry, and therefore the consumer, to pay. Even though not all exactions are legal, many builders do not want the delay and expense of a court battle, and they simply pay the fee.

Municipalities should understand that these practices can discourage builders from investing in community infrastructure because they are wary of additional, unanticipated costs.

A regulatory board's lack of experience and knowledge can have a tremendous impact on community design. As elected or appointed officials, many people serving on planning commissions and municipal councils are not educated or experienced in land-use policy or community design. They respond to plans with individual preconceptions and prejudices. These officials have a responsibility to become educated on the broader issues of design, construction, and finance, and on the specific issues of a proposed community design. As part of this educational process, municipalities should invite the building industry to present ideas and concepts outside of the confines of a specific project. By discussing new ideas without the burden of having to act on a proposal, more open and honest dialogue can take place among everyone involved.

In Lakewood, Colorado, voting members of the planning commission and city council must have completed training before they are allowed to cast a vote. The training includes an in-depth presentation of planning and design issues important to the city. This training helps ensure that the votes cast are informed and educated.

Conflicting desires of the public reveal themselves in an almost schizophrenic manner on a variety of issues. The adage about the two things people hate most—sprawl and density—is a perfect example of how most people approach community development issues. The concepts of closing the door to future development once you have bought a home, of *locally* unacceptable land uses (LULUs), and of build absolutely nothing anywhere near anything (BANANAs) describe in part the public's desire to act in the community interest unless doing so affects individuals' personal interest. An example of this dichotomy is that many Americans believe public transportation can solve some of the crowded highway problems, and yet public transportation use is in a lull. The implication is that public transportation is good as long as someone else uses it.

People's shopping behavior demonstrates a similar attitude. From an aesthetic point of view, most people dislike the architectural character of big-box retail and the sea of cars out front. But, judging by the success of discount stores such as Wal-Mart, people will drive miles out of their way to save a few dollars on 36 rolls of toilet paper. They ignore both the monetary and environmental cost of the additional driving when they are provided with the option to save both time and money on bulk purchases. In aggregate, these decisions affect the quality of life of all residents and contribute to the very things people say they don't like (for example, sprawl, congestion, and pollution).

Another consideration is the public's fear of change. The uncertainty of the unknown is considered a greater threat than the limitations of the status quo. As a result, people protect the status quo with vigor. Making the unknown known, therefore, is absolutely critical. Models, videos, sketches, photographs, and testimonials from people living in similar communities all describe a proposed community better than a set of plans does. Community designers and builders need to reach out to adjacent residents prior to the city's design

review process. An investment in the public's education can help mitigate this issue and build the trust essential to establishing alternative development criteria.

The Public Agency's Perspective

Regulators and approval boards act based on their concerns over how builders and developers approach development. Their impressions are based on past experience as well as on what they may have read or heard. Many look to what a particular builder or developer has built in the past to predict future quality. A quality community builder will seek to understand these concerns and work to mitigate these issues before they become a problem.

A lack of concern for the entire community is often cited as one reason builders should not be allowed to build what they want. A lack of trust, built up over many years, makes cities cautious. City representatives might have the perception that builders or developers just want to make their money and move on to the next community. This perception is heightened when builders resist creating community infrastructure and focus on building the most square footage for the money. To counter this perception, builders should create public spaces within their communities and be active in supporting community events. Extended to the larger community, sponsorship of fundraisers (e.g., Habitat for Humanity, benefits for the local hospital or charity) or broader community-service projects can help restore good will and trust.

Unproven design approaches can make municipalities wary. They know that once the builder or developer leaves, they will be left to provide services and maintain the community. A responsible community builder will help the municipality understand what these costs might be and provide a mechanism to reduce, or eliminate, them. In some communities, for example, the municipality might own and maintain the street, while the Home Owners Association might maintain the alley. In this case, narrower streets might actually cost the city less because there is less public street pavement to maintain, city maintenance responsibility is thereby reduced, and access and parking are not compromised. When there are no driveway cuts to reduce efficiency, parking on one side of the street can provide sufficient parking for homes on both sides. It is up to the community builder to provide the municipality with enough information to address the concerns it may have.

It is reasonable for developers to help develop the systems that will allow the municipality to provide necessary public services. Smaller fire trucks can be subsidized for emergency response on smaller streets, garbage collection can be contracted to a private company when competition ensures the service to customers, and sprinklers may be installed in hard-to-reach homes to reduce the risk for fire damage. In response, the municipalities should embrace new ideas that make sense and can be shown to work.

Insensitivity to the natural environment is a concern municipalities have about builders and developers. Preservation and care of the natural environment is a goal of most communities, and the public strongly supports this goal. To obtain community support for projects, builders and developers should investi-gate environmental issues and develop strategies to minimize or mitigate environmental impacts. To simply ignore environmental impacts or features is to invite trouble in the approval process.

This is not to say that builders or developers should roll over on environmental issues. On the contrary, it suggests that community builders should be knowledgeable about the environmental systems and be prepared to present credible evidence as to why a design approach may be acceptable. They might need to invest in experts to develop an appropriate design approach. They might also need to justify why development may have an impact upon a particular environmental condition, and why this impact should be acceptable. It is also appropriate to challenge the current science of the natural environment. Just as builders should be asked to justify their actions on the environment, so, too, should environmental groups be asked to justify their actions on the built environment. Providing housing for people is important work and all stakeholders should support this work with equal thought and care.

"Greedy developer" is a phrase members of the disgruntled public often mutter at public hearings. Just as in most businesses, some developers are more interested in money than any other quality of their work. Fortunately, these individuals are few. What is interesting is that the public's perception of the leaders of most industries (for example, Michael Dell of Dell Computers) is that they are visionary heroes, creators of jobs, and successful businessmen, while builders and developers are just greedy.

What many people forget is that the place they call home, the school in which their kids learn, the church in which they worship, and the store at which they buy their groceries were likely created by builders and developers. In addition to creating the places where we live our lives, the building industry employs millions of people each year, thus making a significant contribution to our national economy.

Growth doesn't pay its own way is a belief voiced by some. They feel budget pressures are the result of people moving into the community and the subsequent demand for services. They use this argument to justify impact fees for everything from roads to schools. When poorly planned, rapid growth can cause unnecessary demand on public services. This demand is usually the result of too many homes being built before the necessary infrastructure can be put in place. At critical times (for example, when an expanded water or sewer treatment facility is necessary), the cost to provide services can exceed the income derived from development fees and property taxes. Preparing for growth instead of responding to growth would solve many of these problems.

The reality is that balanced residential and commercial growth should result in net revenues for the municipality. Most commercial land uses and higher-density residential uses generate positive cash flow for cities, while low-density, single-family residential uses can be a tax burden, particularly for schools. Unfortunately, most neighbors believe that low-density, single-family housing is a better land use than higher-density, single-family or attached homes. Community builders could

Fiscal Impact Analysis

A simple approach to create a fiscal impact analysis is to first determine the per-capita costs associated with the current municipal budget. This can be done by dividing the budget line items by the number of residents in the municipality. This should be done for each budget item. An analysis of the previous year's per-capita tax revenues should then be completed to determine whether the municipality is operating under a deficit or surplus budget condition. The results of this analysis will determine the sensitivity to additional deficits, or they can underscore the benefits of reducing a deficit or adding to a surplus if the proposed project generates a positive fiscal impact.

Second, it is necessary to determine the potential tax revenues from the proposed project. Proposed sales prices and lot premiums need to be combined for all housing types. If commercial land uses are proposed, tax revenues for those uses must also be estimated. The aggregate value for each land use will be multiplied by the assessed value and the mil levy for each budget line item. This calculation generates a total dollar amount of tax generated for each item in the budget. Next, the estimated population of the proposed project must be determined. It is best to use current municipal statistics for population by housing type. Divide the total revenues by the population to determine tax revenues per capita for the project. This value can than be compared to the per-capita cost of services to determine whether the proposed project is a fiscal benefit or cost.

When growth demands exceed the capability of municipalities to provide infrastructure, the municipal government may be tempted to impose a moratorium on development or impact fees to pay for expansion, or improvement, of needed infrastructure. Both restrictions have significant consequences for builders who have invested in land or planning and are required to pay, or wait. The debate over impact fees can be passionate and loud. If impact fees are imposed, the builder has the legal right to make a direct connection between the impact fee and the necessary improvements. These improvements must benefit the new residents, who ultimately pay the fee.

proactively prepare a *fiscal impact analysis* to demonstrate the actual costs and revenues for their community. A fiscal impact analysis (see above) compares the incremental costs for additional services with the development fee and tax revenue generated by specific uses.

A lack of commitment to quality design and construction is a major complaint associated with sprawling suburban areas—or so say some municipal planning staffs and review bodies. Regulators describe monotonous suburban streets lined with the same stamped-out tract house as evidence that builders do not make a commitment to good design. They decry the approach of large, national builders who build the same floor plan and elevation in communities across the country. Even when builders do make an effort to do a better job, cries of "It's not good enough" can still be heard.

Some builders do not make an attempt to build community. They operate from the belief that the consumer will sacrifice community for more square footage. And in some market segments (generally those representing first-time buyers), this may be true. The long-term problem with this approach is that bad planning reflects poorly on the entire industry, which makes it harder to get any community approved. Developer-initiated design guidelines can have a beneficial impact on the visual quality of the community.

More municipalities are developing their own design guidelines to control the quality of design. In some communities, these guidelines are enforced by competitions for water or sewer taps that essentially force the builders to win a "beauty contest" to proceed. The added costs of additional community features can reduce the affordability of housing. In other communities, the guidelines are enforced as mandatory design standards that leave little flexibility for builders to create their own designs. Unfortunately, the quality of the design is often directly related to the quality of the guidelines. If the guidelines are prepared by municipal staff with little or no design training, the guidelines can actually result in diminished visual quality. It is better for the builder and developer to be proactive and pre-

pare their own guidelines that increase the quality of design in the community and preserve the flexibility that builders need, so they can respond to shifts in market preferences.

Another strategy that several cities have employed is to take on the responsibility of the developer to initiate projects that they believe are desirable. The municipality might work with a group of landowners, assemble the parcel, contract with a design consultant to determine project feasibility and conceptual design, and then go to the marketplace to find a developer interested in building the plan the city has created (Figure 6.3). If completed properly and with the discipline of a developer, this approach can create a vision for large areas of the city and help avoid problems typically associated with piecemeal development. This discipline includes a thorough market-feasibility analysis and design that carefully weigh the costs and benefits of proposed amenities.

Stakeholders in the Community Building Process

Many groups of people not only are a part of the building industry but also have a stake in its success or failure. No-growth attitudes ignore a basic fact: The population of this country continues to grow annually. This growth is from natural population growth and immigration. Natural population growth is in part due to our more advanced healthcare systems and plentiful food. People are staying active and living longer. In spite of concerns over safety and jobs, the country still has a fairly generous immigration policy. From all sources, the national population over the past

Figure 6.3 The city of Westminster, Colorado was the catalyst for development of a mixed-use office and retail project.

10 years has continued to grow at an average annual rate of 3,270,000 people.

In light of this continued population growth, it is important to consider how each stakeholder group is affected by the growth debate. Stakeholder groups include builders and developers, and, by association, the myriad of businesses that are involved in the building industry. Carpenters, plumbers, electricians, drywall contractors, carpet and tile layers, truck drivers, and landscapers are all directly affected by residential and commercial construction. Those in support industries are also affected. These groups include financial institutions, furniture manufacturers, lumber mills, plant nurseries, appliance manufacturers, and all the retail-sales operations that distribute and sell these goods and the home itself.

A large part of our nation's economy is linked to community building. A recent report by the National Association of Home Builders ("Housing: The Key to Economic Recovery," 2003) states that approximately 3.8 million people are employed in industries related to community building, and these people generate approximately $1,496 billion in annual expenditures, or approximately 14 percent of the gross domestic product. Additionally, the industry pays more than $66 billion annually in federal, state, and local tax revenues and fees.

The general public is also a primary stakeholder. As buyers, they must live with the results for decades to come. They are concerned with the quality of construction, the design and function of the house and community, price, and resale value. Each of these concerns is interconnected. Failure to address any one concern can create a negative image for builders. If community builders want to be in business for some time, it is important that they adequately address all of these concerns.

The regulators, including municipal planning and engineering staffs, planning commissions, city councils, or county boards, are by extension representatives of the general public. They share the same concerns; in addition, they are charged with ensuring public safety and welfare. Another charge is that of maintenance of public improvements. Often, this responsibility seems to override others because most municipalities do not have sufficient budgets to perform all of the required maintenance. These maintenance responsibilities include public improvements built by community builders as well as those built by the municipality. Over time, this deferred maintenance requires significant improvements to existing infrastructure to accommodate future growth.

Few communities have the discipline to tax themselves to adequately maintain the improvements and public land dedications they require.

In February 2001, the *Los Angeles Times* reported that in California alone decades of disinvestments in infrastructure would require an estimated $8-billion to $100-billion investment to bring the existing infrastructure back to a point at which it would maintain an expected quality of life. The article, "New Crises Loom in State's Aging Infrastructure" (by Marla Dickerson and Stuart Silverstein), indicated that delays caused by traffic congestion as a result of poor infrastructure cost each person of driving age nearly $1,400 annually, or more than $12.4 billion in total. This cost creates a disincentive for residents and businesses that might want to become a part of the community, and it reduces the quality of life for existing residents.

Environmentalists, and the natural systems they represent, have a significant interest in growth. Environmentalists believe that many species are indicator species, in that, as a particular species declines or is threatened or endangered, these trends indicate more severe damage to the ecosystem. This damage will diminish the quality of life we now enjoy and eventually endanger the human species. It is essential for community builders to respect natural systems as much as practical.

It is also important for environmental groups to recognize that the builders of our communities perform a valuable function. The concerns for the environment must be balanced with the interests of people. Trade-offs should be made in a reasonable and deliberate manner. Community builders should incorporate environmental features into the community as much as possible. When negative environmental impact is unavoidable, techniques should be explored to mitigate those impacts. Wetland mitigation banking is one strategy to provide functional wetlands to replace those that needed to be filled. Some environmental groups question the viability of wetland mitigation banking. In an effort to find workable solutions to current problems, environmental and building-industry groups should jointly fund long-term experimental techniques.

Several programs speak to the cooperation between the building industry and environmentalists. The Building With Trees program is one such program. Sponsored by The Arbor Day Foundation and the National Association of Home Builders. this program encourages builders to incorporate trees, and proper tree maintenance, in the design of their communities (Figure 6.4). The awards given to builders who excel in that regard communicate to buyers the sensitivity that has been given to community design.

The Approval Process

An effective approval process is composed of several important steps. They include the following:

1. A complete site analysis and an assessment of the neighborhood attitudes.
2. Presentation of the site analysis and market realities to individual neighborhood groups.
3. Preparation and refinement of alternate concept ideas.
4. Presentation of the site analysis and concept ideas to the city.
5. Separate meetings with individual neighborhood groups to present concept ideas.
6. Incorporation of neighbor and city comments into a refined preliminary concept plan that addresses the issues and concerns of both.
7. Attendance at planning-commission and city-council hearings prior to submitting the concept plan for approval, to gain a clear understanding of city issues, concerns, and vision for growth.
8. Engagement in a city workshop process with key staff and officials to review preliminary thoughts and ideas.

Figure 6.4 Saving trees enhances the value of the community.

9. Resolution of all issues prior to hearings.
10. Avoidance of attempts to resolve disagreements in the public hearing.
11. Request for the approval.

Preparing a complete site analysis allows the community designer to make a direct connection between the site opportunities and constraints and the design. Without a logical link, the design may appear arbitrary, and the reviewers may feel free to modify the design. Understanding neighbors' attitudes upfront reduces the potential of incorporating controversial features into the plan. If the plan is predisposed to alleviate neighborhood concerns, it will be better received throughout the process.

Different neighborhood groups will have different issues. If presentations are made jointly, the different groups may quarrel amongst themselves and compete for the community designer's attention to resolve their individual issues. Separating the groups allows the community designer to focus on each group's problem without interference. Separate presentations also keep potential opponents from each group from coming together to form a *splinter group*. Splinter groups are not representative of the entire neighborhood's position and can cause problems at hearings.

With information gleaned from these meetings with the neighborhood groups, it is possible to develop concept ideas that build in potential solutions to neighborhood issues. Designers and builders who do this indicate that they have been listening to the concerns of the groups, and that they are working to mitigate those concerns as much as possible. When it is not possible to mitigate a concern, a reason needs to be communicated to the group involved. Reviewing the concept ideas with the city before going back to the neighborhood gives the community designer the benefit of the city's position on key issues that may have an impact on the design. If this position is opposite that of the neighborhood group's position, then the community designer can let the city defend its position and remain neutral on the outcome.

Attending planning-commission or city-council hearings prior to preparing the submittal helps the community designer understand individual preferences key members may have. These preferences should be woven into the community plan to elicit positive feedback, if possible, from each member. Even if preferences are not included in the plan, it is important to understand how each member reacts to various plan elements, each member's approach to questions, and his or her voting trend. This understanding can help the community designer prepare a presentation strategy for the hearings.

When possible, resolving all outstanding issues before going to the hearing is important. Unless it is impossible to give on a particular issue, being prepared and able to do so is important; discussions on unresolved issues have a tendency to generate greater scrutiny of the plan, which can raise even more issues. Designers and builders need to determine their fallback position before the hearing and enact it if the discussion seems to be going against the plan as submitted. Trying to find solutions to problems at the time of the hearing creates confusion and usually results in delays.

And in the end, ask for the approval. So often, after serious presentations and discussions, the planning commission or city council members can be confused by the proceedings, and they appreciate hearing again exactly what you want them to do. If interpretation is left to the planning staff, they may misinterpret what you want. Make sure they understand.

Eight Tips for More Effective Processing

1. **Begin with good design and a well-conceived and well-documented community story.** This seems obvious, but given the number of communities that are delayed or not even approved, the message is not getting out. Review agencies want to see the best community design you can afford to create. The community story must be well-documented and effectively presented. It is important to bring the emotion of the community to the presentation.

2. **Employ critical thinking.** When you are developing a presentation strategy, thinking like an attorney is beneficial. Think ahead several steps to determine what might go wrong, and prepare an approach to counter the problems. Be logical and concise. Sometimes it is better to counter the emotional presentations of neighbors with cool logic supported by the emotion of the community story rather than by any particular issue.

3. **Do your homework.** It is better to be over-prepared than under-prepared. Not having a key graphic or piece of evidence can cause you to lose on a key issue. Research built communities locally and nationally. Be prepared to supply planning-commission or city-council members with copies of reports, photographs, or studies.

4. **Develop a relationship with staff.** It is easier to communicate with people you know and like. Get to know the people and their interests. Be respectful and courteous. Stand up for you rights, but be fair and reasonable. Save the heated discussions for private. Criticizing a friend in public is not appropriate. When someone helps you achieve an approval, thank him or her, and send a letter to let the planning director know how you feel.

5. **Good graphics are critical.** The saying "A picture is worth a thousand words" holds true for presentations to laypeople. The graphics need to tell the story. They should be bold and readable from the back of the room. Photos and sketches are great. Show previous project sketches and the built community; these bring a realism to the new sketches and give the reviewer the confidence the community will look like what you say it will look like.

6. **Respond thoroughly to all issues.** In a written summary prepared before the hearing, make sure you have addressed every issue you know of. When you are compromising on an issue, make sure the city knows it. When you disagree, explain why you disagree, and give supporting documentation.

7. **Describe the features and benefits of the community.** The municipality wants to know what it will get in return for project approval. Take the time to explain how the community design meets city goals and objectives. List the project features and how they benefit the city and the future residents.

8. **Remember, a lot of design happens during the approval process.** The inevitable negotiations and problem solving that are part of the approval process represent an opportunity to refine and influence the community design. You must be willing to be involved in the process or let others manipulate the design. It is better to achieve the essence of your design than capitulate the final decision to others. Such compromising requires builders to know what they can afford to lose and what should remain.

Processing the community design to ensure that it meets the original design intent is a vital function of the community designer. Without careful planning and strategy, the project may falter, or, worse yet, be denied. Ensuring that the design ideas are not diluted by the process is important work. Creative thinking and perseverance usually result in success.

CHAPTER 7
Paying for Community

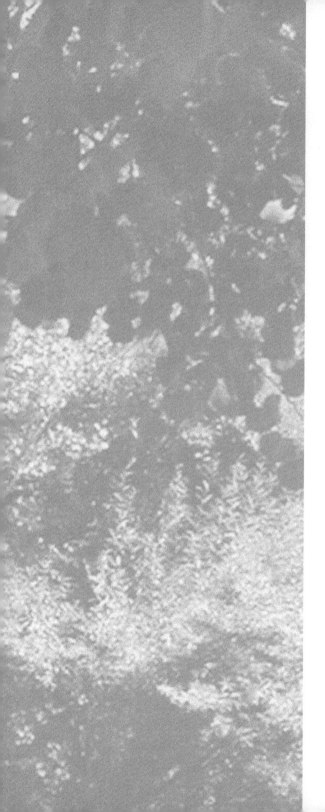

Compared to building traditional subdivisions, building community requires an expanded approach to development and building budgets. Community builders understand the value they create through their investment in creating a sense of community, and they use that value to balance additional costs. This value is expressed through sales pace and price, neighborhood acceptance, and faster approvals. They capitalize on this value by building the idea of community into their discussions with regulators, the press, and neighbors, making it a part of their public image, and blending it into all of their advertising. Community life becomes an identifying brand for the educated community builder and a competitive advantage in the marketplace.

In contrast, traditional subdividers compete primarily on the basis of price. To compete effectively on price, developer/builders must create as many lots as possible to amortize land and site-development costs (Figure 7.1). They minimize, or eliminate, common open spaces and amenities because these take up land that could be used for more lots, and they add Home Owners Association fees that burden homeowners. Where possible, they ignore natural features to make room for even more lots. Location is not as important as raw-land cost. Builders can sell more square footage for less money.

A major flaw of this pricing strategy is that the marketplace has room for only one "cheapest" builder. A special land deal, lax regulations, or even substandard construction can have an impact on the cost advantage from project to project. Larger builders may enter the market and undermine local pricing through volume discounts for materials and labor. Another flaw in this approach is that the public, and the regulators who are empowered to protect the public good, respond negatively to this type of growth. It may be possible to make quick profits on one development, at the expense

155

Figure 7.1 Buyers immediately sense when the idea of community is just hype.

of delayed approvals and significantly lower profits for subsequent projects. This is, at best, a risky long-term business model.

Many builders are hesitant to make the necessary investment to build community because little guidance is available on how much to spend, what to spend it on, and how the investment will be repaid. As a result, many make only a half-hearted attempt at creating community, and they don't achieve the returns they expected. The purpose of this chapter is to outline the benefits of investing in community, to help the community builder evaluate how much should be invested, and to outline strategies for funding the investment. Development programming and phasing, pro-forma and cash-flow analysis, and business strategies are also discussed as tools to help the community builder be successful.

The Benefits of Investing in Community

Investing in community yields both tangible and intangible benefits. The tangible benefits include greater sales traffic, higher per-foot retail prices, and faster sales pace. The intangible benefits include greater short-term and long-term public acceptance of community development, and enhanced value in future phases, future communities, and company reputation.

When a builder effectively communicates a community story, people are likely to notice. The press is more inclined to publish positive stories about a community that relates to the history of the area, responds to the site and environment, and promotes interaction among the residents, than an ordinary project that sells a lot of homes. A compelling community story can bring continued coverage, resulting in more than one article covering more than one element of the community (Figure 7.2). For example, one story might discuss an educational program that takes advantage of the nature trail, while another might discuss how a diversity of housing makes it possible for more people serving the community to own homes there. The following actions help the press endorse the community, which raises buyers' awareness of community features and results in greater sales traffic:

- The developer/builder proactively develops article ideas for the press.
- Story ideas revolve around special community design features and potential community events.
- Stories primarily promote the community and only indirectly promote the builder.
- Each story describes a benefit for the larger community.
- Each story incorporates the community vision.

In most cases, creating a sense of community does cost more. Protecting natural areas, building amenities, and establishing community programs all require an investment of both time and money. Proper community design "value-engineers" expense by taking advantage of the site's natural features. When additional expenses arise, designers/builders

Figure 7.2 Newspaper headlines can raise awareness of the community.

should consider several strategies that mitigate costs. Most important is the opportunity to charge lot premiums for enhanced lots within the community. The most valuable premiums are adjacent to community amenities; however, when properly designed, community amenities yield premiums throughout the community (Figure 7.3). Shared amenities bring value to every homeowner, not just to a few lots. In addition, the amenities become

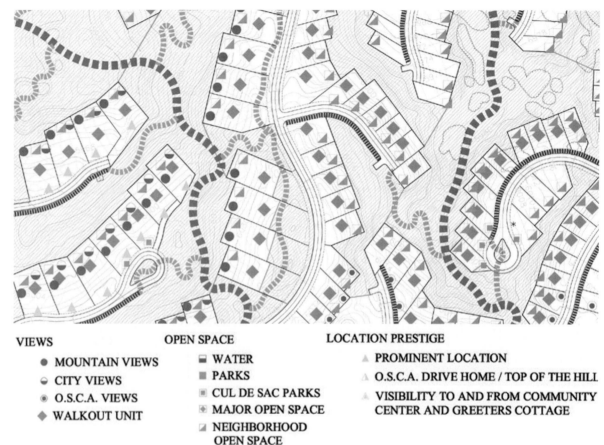

VIEWS

- ● MOUNTAIN VIEWS
- ◡ CITY VIEWS
- ◉ O.S.C.A. VIEWS
- ◆ WALKOUT UNIT

OPEN SPACE

- ▪ WATER
- ▪ PARKS
- ▪ CUL DE SAC PARKS
- ✚ MAJOR OPEN SPACE
- ◹ NEIGHBORHOOD
  OPEN SPACE

LOCATION PRESTIGE

- ▲ PROMINENT LOCATION
- △ O.S.C.A. DRIVE HOME / TOP OF THE HILL
- ◭ VISIBILITY TO AND FROM COMMUNITY
  CENTER AND GREETERS COTTAGE

Figure 7.3 Lot premiums increase total revenues.

part of, and enrich, the community story. The graphic in Figure 7.3 illustrates how lot premiums may be calculated for an open-space-amenity community.

Another strategy is to simply charge more per square foot for the lot or home. This approach requires that the builder educate buyers as to why one community design is better than another. The greater the number of community features and programs, the easier

this is. Related to this strategy is the opportunity to increase sales prices as the community amenities are built. Additionally, building some amenities early in the development gives buyers a high level of assurance that all of the amenities will be built as promised. Simply planting larger trees and completing land-scaped areas can also have an affordable and immediate positive impact on pricing (Figure 7.4).

Figure 7.4 Planting 3-inch to 4-inch trees has an immediate positive impact on community character.

A third strategy is to reduce the size of the lot and/or home in order to reduce other, non-amenity costs and keep the overall price competitive. One approach is to diversify housing type to increase the density, which allows the builder to amortize the costs over more units.

This approach adds to the texture of the community, expands the potential market, and increases the absorption rate. Community amenities do create a rationale for increased density; however, it is important to keep in mind that some municipalities are opposed to increased density. Another approach is to reduce the size of homes, which requires buyers to make a trade-off of space for community amenities. This approach can be very successful with more sophisticated buyers with whom quality is more important than square footage.

Within any price range, a well-designed community will outperform a poorly designed community. Each additional home helps complete the vision for the community and adds value. Buyers are drawn to a sense of community and want to be part of the activity. Faster sales benefit the community builder by reducing costs. These reduced costs include financing costs (the builder doesn't need to carry the infrastructure costs as long), marketing and advertising costs (the total number of weeks of advertising, and the sales staff, are reduced), and operations costs (salaried superintendents can move on to the next community sooner). These reduced costs begin to offset the potential increase in costs for amenities, and together the benefits outweigh the costs, resulting in better profits and less long-term risk.

Intangible short-term benefits are realized when neighbors and regulators support the community. They appreciate the extra effort to design a community that respects the neighbors and site context. They understand that the higher value of a well-designed community will have a positive impact on adjacent property values as well. Long-term benefits are achieved as municipalities associate the community builder with quality design and construction (Figure 7.5). The community builder will be welcomed back for future developments.

Although it is important for builders to distinguish themselves on quality and design, it also is important to remember to match community amenities with what buyers can afford.

Over time, well-designed and well-constructed communities appreciate faster. This appreciation should be communicated to buyers so they understand the benefit of this investment. Builders should track resale prices as part of their marketing efforts and demonstrate this appreciation to potential buyers. The increase in value will also be realized by the builder's own company. A solid reputation will significantly enhance the value of the "good will" portion of the company asset.

How Much to Invest in Building Community

The most important influence in determining how much to invest in community is the realization that building community is as much a part of the development cost as roads, water, and sewer. This cost needs to be budgeted upfront and balanced with the other costs of development. Because the buyer perceives this investment more than "nonvisible" improvements (such as sewer and water lines), the return on dollars invested is maximized. Preliminary cost estimates based on the community vision help the builder understand what the total cost may be. Once a development budget has been established, it can be compared to the expected revenues to determine

Figure 7.5 Well-executed amenities and landscaped areas result in rapid appreciation.

profitability. Fine-tuning the budget ensures an appropriate profit for the anticipated risk.

Industry averages are a good place to begin in determining how much to spend on creating community. These averages should be modified to reflect the specific community situation. The resulting pro-forma analysis represents the project as completed. This differs from a cash-flow analysis in that the pro-forma analysis is a snapshot in time versus an analysis over time. Each analysis has a valuable role to play in evaluating the potential success or failure of a particular community design. The pro-forma analysis depicts the general performance of the community by comparing total project costs to total project revenues.

Pro Forma Analysis (as a percentage of total revenues for home and lots sales)

Raw land and improvements	20% to 25%
Raw land	7% to 10%
Site development	8% to 14%
Landscape and amenities	2% to 5%
Indirect construction and fees	2% to 4%
Direct construction	50% to 55%
Marketing and sales	4% to 7%
Financing	2% to 3%
General administration	5% to 8%
Profit	8% to 12%

Note: The expected profit stated above is appropriate for the home and lot combined. Profit for community development and lot sales ranges only from 25 percent to 40 percent.

Because building community is part of the marketing strategy for the community, a portion of the marketing budget should be earmarked for community and *soft infrastructure*. Generally, soft infrastructure, or community programs, should be financed from the marketing budget. *Hard infrastructure* costs (open spaces, and amenities) are typically financed from the landscape and amenities budget. If a particular budget item appears to be underfunded, it may be necessary to reevaluate product mix, pricing, or unit size to bring the budget to a level that is appropriate for the community.

Analyzing the budget breakdowns for the nation's top 20 builders and the next 100 builders is instructive (*Professional Builder*, 2003). It is important to remember that, for the most part, these builders compete on price, and their investment in community is generally less than that of the smaller builder who needs to offer community amenities to remain competitive. These averages are based on the retail price of the home and lot combined.

The cost advantages of being a large builder are apparent: Direct construction costs

Category	Industry Averages	Top 20	Next 100
Raw land	7% to 10%	8.9%	9%
Site development	8% to 14%	14.6%	11.1%
Landscape/amenities	2% to 5%	.6%	1.3%
Indirect construction and fees	2% to 4%	2%	3.3%
Direct construction	50% to 55%	48.4%	50.8%
Marketing/sales	4% to 7%	5.1%	5.7%
Financing	2% to 3%	1.7%	2.9%
General administration	5% to 8%	6.1%	5.9%
Profit	8% to 12%	12.6%	10%

(bricks and sticks) and financing costs are significantly lower. These lower costs can be attributed to greater buying power for materials and supplies, and cash from stock offerings. What is also apparent is the low funding for landscape and amenities. These realities suggest that a good strategy to compete in markets in which large builders are present is to develop a strong sense of community with targeted amenities. Community builders should purchase land wisely, keep their administration costs low, and invest in building community to compete with larger builders.

Cash-Flow Analysis

The purpose of a cash-flow analysis is to evaluate a specific plan over time and test assumptions relating to financing, phasing, timing of improvements, and loan requirements. For example, it is possible to determine whether developing community amenities early is justified by faster sales and additional premium income. It is also possible to balance development phasing with revenues to ensure that there is enough income to pay for basic infrastructure. A cash-flow analysis will also identify the maximum loan amount that will be needed, when it will be needed, and the total cost of financing.

To maximize the effectiveness of a cash-flow analysis, replicating the actual development sequence in as much detail as possible is necessary. Assumptions of costs and revenues displayed monthly or quarterly in a spreadsheet can be used to calculate *return on investment (ROI)*, and the *discounted rate of return* (Figure 7.6). The ROI compares the real-estate investment to other uses of funds, while the discounted rate of return expresses the value of future revenues in today's dollars. The following list illustrates typical line items in a detailed cash-flow analysis:

Net Revenues by Time Period

Return on Investment

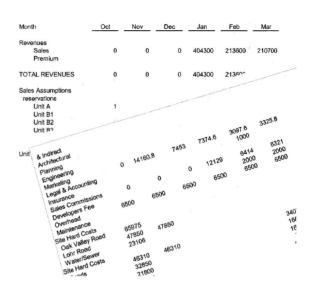

Figure 7.6 A typical cash-flow analysis.

Discounted Rate of Return

Revenues
- Revenues by product type and time period
- Additional revenues, including land sales, HOA fees, or lot premiums
- Total revenues

Costs
- Land costs through purchase or options
- Site-development costs by phase (for all major components including roads, water, sewer, grading, dry utilities, etc.)
- Amenity costs by phase
- Direct construction costs, with various assumptions of per-foot costs
- Marketing costs, including model-home complexes, collateral material, and fees

- Indirect construction costs, including design and permit fees
- General and administrative costs
- Financing costs, including terms

Special District Financing

In some states, enabling legislations provides for the creation of metropolitan districts or special districts to fund infrastructure improvements, including landscape and amenities. Special districts are created to finance one specific item (such as a water system), while metropolitan districts finance two or more items. This infrastructure can include roads, water, sewer, landscape, and amenities. Design fees and maintenance costs can also be provided from district revenues. A district service plan is created that describes those costs and services paid for by the district, and the method and timing of repaying those funds.

District financing involves selling quasi-municipal bonds backed by a mil levy (an amount of tax per $1,000 of assessed value) on real estate within the district. Depending on the fiscal stability of the municipality, interest rates are often less than what might be available in the commercial lending arena. These districts reduce a municipality's bonding capacity and therefore must be approved by the municipality. As a result, the municipality will require the community builder to demonstrate significant public features and benefits related to the bond approval. Not coincidentally, these features and benefits are the same that help create a sense of community.

A similar form of financing is the Tax Increment Financing, or TIF, district. The premise of a TIF district is that district bonds are repaid from the difference in tax rate, the increment, between the undeveloped land and the improved land within the district. Because most residential land does not generate a significant tax increment (once school mil levies have been removed), TIF is usually reserved for commercial property. If the community development includes a commercial component, the community builder should investigate the potential of blending financing mechanisms within the same development.

Another strategy to pay for community is to share in the expense by forming an alliance with another, noncompeting builder. Each builder participates in the community design, determines what housing type and market segment he or she wishes to build for, and contributes to the community amenities on a prorated basis. The actual participation should be adjusted to reflect the difference in price points of the specific product and the match between the amenities and the market desires. This approach can result in the amenities and programs necessary to create community that, alone, each builder would have been unable to achieve.

Understanding the relationship between costs and revenues helps builders minimize risk and enhance value. Building community helps meet both objectives. Building community reduces risk by speeding sales and creating additional financing opportunities. It enhances the value of the homes within the community.

It results in communities that have a competitive advantage based on desirable characteristics. People want to live in well-designed communities.

CHAPTER 8
Marketing Community

Marketing the community is an exciting and fulfilling journey focused on telling the community story. The marketing begins during the site analysis and the creation of the community vision, long before the first home is ready to sell. Opportunities exist at each step of the design and approval process to communicate the community story to the press, regulators, neighbors, and potential buyers. Effective community marketing seizes each opportunity and extends the impact. It is important to remember that being a community builder requires dedication to the details. Marketing is as important as the business and design elements of building community. Community builders should use all appropriate marketing strategies, including press releases, community parties, collateral materials, and building the vision, to communicate the community story. This chapter concludes with a discussion of the importance of marketing community life and cost-effective community programs.

Press Releases

During the design process, several unique community features may emerge. These features should reflect local traditions, site context, or site features. Such features can become the nucleus of the community story, and they present an opportunity to inform the buying public. The community-design team can help determine what opportunities exist and are appropriate for a press release. Seek out the opportunities to create win/win situations that build good will. Write press releases with an eye on communicating the entire community story as well as the individual feature. If you don't write the story and control the content, it may be written for you, and you will have no control over the final copy and the resulting perception. Make sure to follow through with the story and provide regular updates. Once the members of the press realize that you are a credible source of interesting stories, they will be more inclined to run subsequent press releases.

Determining what is worthy of a press release depends on the nature of the community story and the impact of a specific feature. A decision to save a stand of trees might be expanded into a joint project for a local university forestry program. The students could inventory and study the trees and then establish a tree-thinning plan and tree-maintenance guidelines for the Home Owners Association. A headline reading "Local Builder Works with the University to Save Trees" can pay dividends throughout the approval and sales process. In larger projects, land set aside for a future phase might become a temporary plant nursery, giving students an opportunity for hands-on training while the project grows plants for eventual transplant into the rest of the community.

Service projects are great community-interest stories. Having the community sponsor a charity event, such as a 5K run, softball game, or silent auction, shines the spotlight on the community and allows the builder to tell the community story. Sponsoring these events in conjunction with a local television station or newspaper garners ongoing publicity. Find a way to weave the community story into the event. For example, an equestrian community with a ranch theme might sponsor a tricycle rodeo, or an open-space community on a lake might support a regatta. For a community with a wonderful trail system, a charity run might be appropriate.

Community Parties

A relatively inexpensive strategy to inform buyers about the community is to host a community party. The intent is to invite potential buyers and realtors, allow them to have a good time, and at the same time learn about the vision for the community. This party can be as simple as erecting a large tent on site and grilling burgers and hot dogs, or as elegant as a catered event with entertainment. Completing an amenity, opening a new filing of homes, and wanting to encourage new neighbors to meet are all good reasons to have a party. Be creative to maximize the exposure for each event.

Realtors can be a terrific source for potential buyers and should be encouraged to participate in the sales of the community. Offering incentives for referrals that result in sales are effective when there are on-site sales staff, but do not turn over the job of informing the buyer about the features and benefits of the community. On-site sales people are trained to promote the community benefits, while referring realtors may not have such training. When no on-site sales staff are available, consider offering training sessions to the local realtor community. Realtors need to understand the community story and the unique selling propositions of the community.

Beginning with the invitations, multiple opportunities exist from each party for publicity and story telling. The invitation should relate to the community story and highlight special community features. An ice-cream social with entertainment might draw people interested in buying in a traditional neighborhood, while a clam bake might support the image of a waterfront community. The party

Figure 8.1 Renderings can communicate the feeling of the community.

Credit: Courtesy of DTJ Design.

can be held adjacent to an existing natural-site feature, at a model home, or at a community park. The atmosphere should be festive, fun, and lively.

One builder in Fort Collins, Colorado solicits help from his consultants and suppliers to provide the hospitality service at the party. The mortgage banker serves food, while the landscape contractor serves drinks. In exchange for their services, each vendor is introduced to potential customers. Design consultants are available to communicate the community story and answer any questions prospective buyers may have. This arrangement helps defray the cost of the party. When this same builder is selling high-end homes, he or she creates a DVD invitation that illustrates the community amenities and tells the community story. The reality is that new buyers become the best sale people for the community when they talk to their friends about the wonderful events that happen in their new neighborhood and urge them to become part of a special place.

Collateral Materials

All communities will benefit from a community sales office. The community story must be displayed, and sales staff must present it. This can be done through sketches, plans, and models (Figure 8.1). The marketing director, assisted by the community designer, should train the sales staff on the community story. If the community represents multiple builders, the primary sales office should be used to pre-qualify buyers, tell them the community story, and direct them to the appropriate housing type or price range.

Within the community sales office should be a *topo table* that illustrates the entire community. This display gives the salesperson the opportunity to talk about the community's features and benefits. Lifestyle photographs help buyers visualize living in the community and using the amenities. Handouts that include floor plans and price lists should be expanded to include the community story.

In addition to the community story, a description of community features should be included in the take-home packet. Informational sheets should describe how special features have been incorporated into the community design, and how residents can help care for the community. For example, a map showing a wetland boardwalk may describe the various wetland plants that can be found along the way. The text could go on to explain how residents can protect the waterway by reducing fertilizers or properly disposing of oils and paints. This approach communicates the builder's sensitivity to the environment and the importance of working together to protect the community.

Many builders create clothing and coffee mugs with the company logo. These items keep the builder's name foremost in the buyers' minds. Builders should consider expanding this notion of *branding* to include the community logo and name. Buyers can be given shirts or hats that display the community name. The clothing can be tailored to the project story. The equestrian community might give out jean shirts with the community logo

to buyers, while a golf community would give out golf shirts. Use of this apparel builds a pride in belonging and acts as a living billboard. When asked, buyers will usually extol the virtues of living in the community.

Another successful strategy is to surprise buyers with small gifts when they move in. As part of the prequalification process, buyers can complete a survey that asks, among other things, about several of their favorite items. The options might include the women's perfume, favorite color, and toothpaste, or the men's favorite beer or wine. On move-in, the buyers find the right beer in the refrigerator, toothbrushes and toothpaste in the bathroom, and perfume next to the bathroom sink. These small gifts extend a personal touch to buyers and become the focus of their conversations with friends for months to come.

The purpose of marketing the community is to expand to as many friends of the new residents as possible the effort you make with one successful sale. People begin to think about moving when their friends move. They want to stay connected to their friends. They want to be a part of the excitement and buzz of a new community. Capturing as many of those potential buyers as possible is important.

Building the Vision

Early on in the construction process, buyers need to be comfortable that all of the community amenities will be built as described. They believe the community story and can't wait to see it become a reality. Building as much up front as financially feasible will provide the comfort level necessary to turn prospects into buyers. The saying "You only have one opportunity to make a good first impression" is especially true in building community. Amenities important to the community story must be budgeted for early construction. Doing this builds on the marketing efforts and enhances sales. Focus on design details to obtain the most value from the amenity. For example, in areas in which people will gather, use masonry or other "high touch" materials, or create a fine texture with flowers or sculpture to add interest and credibility. Do not dismiss this opportunity to build trust with the public. Make sure that the community delivers on every promise made during marketing and sales efforts.

When you can't afford to build a community amenity immediately, you should still highlight the community features. A large color rendering of the amenity with expected construction dates tells buyers what to expect and when. Another option is to create a whimsical sign that tells a story about the feature. At Brighton Crossing, Carma Colorado developed interesting characters to explain future community amenities (Figure 8.2). This approach replaced the traditional community sales office, which reduced the developer's initial investment while it continued to communicate the community features and benefits. A large bee announces, "All these parks and gardens, where do I start?" A handout describing the feature is tucked into a real-estate curb box for visitors to take with them. This strategy helps tell the community story even when potential buyers don't have a sales office to stop in. Potential buyers can't resist getting information from the box, especially because there is no sales person who might pressure them into buying, and everyone wants to collect information and scrutinize it at his or her leisure.

Figure 8.2 At Brighton Crossing, a whimsical sign describes the many parks.

Figure 8.3 Lifestyle signs appeal to the target market.

A sign of a commitment to quality is outstanding landscaping. Use larger trees and shrubs to give buyers the impression that the community is well-established. Large shrub beds can act as visual screens and define outdoor spaces. Insist that the landscape display color and texture. The landscape should enhance the image of the community. Design hardscape elements and street furniture that support the community story.

Another method used to communicate future built amenities is to place signs that communicate an anticipated lifestyle at the model-home complex (Figure 8.3). These signs should visually describe the events that can occur in the community and act as reinforcement to the salesperson's message. The signs should be easy to read because they will be viewed by both walkers visiting model homes and drive-by traffic. Figure 8.4 illustrates effective lifestyle sign marketing.

Community Life

The community comes to life when people share activities and develop friendships. The connections people make during these activities and events build a true sense of community. The community designer can create the places for community events to occur; however, the people who live in the community must eventually organize and manage these events. The builder or developer can initially encourage social interaction by facilitating community events that will, over time, be the responsibility of the Home Owners Association or group of neighbors.

Many events are relatively simple to organize and sponsor. They should be designed to build community life. In the spring, the events might include gardening seminars by a local master gardener, bird-watching lectures, an Easter egg hunt, or even a street market. The summer events might include neighborhood-wide garage sales (organized and advertised by the builder), a community "fun" and picnic, or a fishing derby. Fall might bring a pumpkin festival (at which the builder purchases a truckload of pumpkins and hosts a pumpkin-carving contest) or composting lectures, while the winter is perfect for community caroling and exhibits by resident artists. A babysitting co-op can be created in a community that is designed to appeal to young families.

Many of these events are inexpensive to sponsor, yet the impact is tremendous. The builder needs to develop a written set of guidelines for each event and pass those guidelines on to the community. The guidelines need to be developed only once, and then they can be used over and over again to amortize the cost over several communities and make their development affordable. They can be packaged to appear specific to each community, which adds to the special nature of the event.

Independently, these marketing strategies will have a positive impact on sales. Together, they have even greater impact. Builders should utilize as many strategies as possible to ensure that visitors become prospects and, eventually, buyers. The pro-forma analysis should provide sufficient budget for community events. Builders should consider creating a position in their companies specifically for someone to create and monitor community-building activities. As the community becomes a desirable place to live, community builders will be repaid in faster sales and higher prices.

Glossary

Alley-loaded. Homes that have garage access from an alley located at the rear of the home.

Bioswale. A shallow drainage designed to remove impurities from run-off prior to the water entering a larger water body. The impurities are removed by sedimentation (slowing the water enough to allow precipitation of larger particles) and plants. Plant species are chosen that absorb phosphates and nitrates, two primary causes of algae growth and subsequent reduction of dissolved oxygen in water.

Eyebrow. Generally half of a cul-de-sac with island forming a semi-circular access to homes around the outside.

Infill. Development on sites that are surrounded by existing development with public services nearby.

Motor Court/Court Cluster. A group of attached, or detached homes facing an internal driveway that provides access to garages and parking spaces. The court typically has a land-scaped island, parking, or both in the center. |The drive around the court is typically a private drive where each home owner shares in the maintenance.

Niche Builder. A builder that specializes in creating homes and/or communities that appeal to a small segment of the market.

Pinwheel Cluster. A group of attached homes (usually 4 or less) where the front of each units faces outwardly in a different direction than the other units. Private, outdoor space is usually either at the front of each home or to the side.

Stub Street. A short (150 feet +/−) public street without a turn-around at the end.

Suburban Sprawl. A derogatory term given to unchecked growth characterized by mostly single family detached homes on large lots, significant numbers of the same type of housing, and segregated uses on large tracts of previously undeveloped land in the suburbs.

Water quality ponds. Ponds designed to remove, through sedimentation, large particles including heavy metals and silt.

Zero Lot Line. A type of single family detached home where one side of the home has a zero setback from the property line so that the other side may have a more useable yard space.

Additional Reading

A Better Place to Live: Reshaping the American Suburb, Phillip Langdon, University of Massachusetts Press, reprint edition, 1997.

Community Preferences: What the Buyers Really Want in Design, Features, and Amenities, AmericanLIVES, Inc., 1999.

Consumer Behavior Applications to Real Estate, Gibler and Nelson, 1998.

Land Development, 9th Edition, Linda Kone, BuilderBooks, 1999.

Lifestyle Market Research for the Design of Production Houses, Noble, 2000.

The Great Good Place, 3rd Edition, Ray Oldenburg, Marlowe & Company, 1999.

Index

The Village at Autumn Lake (WI) example, 119–22, 123
Community investment benefits, 156–60
Community leaders, xviii
Community life
  design integrating, 99–101
  marketing impact, 171
Community parties, 166–67, 171
Community stories, 88
  amenities and, 88
  defined, 83
  lake village example, 83–85
  market desires and, 88
Community types, 108
Community values/perceptions, 65–68
Community visioning, 79–96
  adjacent land use and, 62–64, 88–90
  amenities in, 85–88
  budgeting for, 91
  Colorado ranch vision, 82–83, 84
  community stories and. *See* Community stories
  controlling. *See* Design guidelines
  defined, 79, 80
  examples, 80–90
  historical Wisconsin vision, 80–82
  HOAs and, 91
  marketing, 168–71
  as place making, 80
  planning for, 90–91
  summary vision document, 90–91
  value of, 79, 91
  Wisconsin lake village vision, 83–88
Concept ideas, 103–4
Condominium(s), 27
  diversity and, 119
  example community, 130
  flexibility, 39

market segments, 24
  types of, 24, 35–36, 37
Consumer preferences, 20, 21, 26
Country Club District (MO), 10
Court clusters, 31, 33, 173
Cumbernauld (Scotland), 9, 12–13
Curb under-drains, 4–5
Cut and fill, 15

D

Deed restrictions, 10
Demographic indicators, 19
Density
  home value and, 35
  increasing, 36, 118–19
  low levels, 59, 145
  threshold, 34
Density (high), 37, 113
  advantages, 145
  amenities rationalizing, 159
  public conflicts, 142–43
  reducing perception of, 116, 117, 128
  tradeoffs, 122, 142–43
Design drivers, 101–3
Design guidelines
  architecture guidelines, 92–94, 93
  CC & Rs vs., 92
  contents, 92–93
  controlling vision, 91–96
  as fun, informative, 94–95
  introduction, 92
  landscape guidelines, 93, 94
  purpose of, 91–92, 94, 96
  site planning guidelines, 92
  Tallyn's Reach example, 94–97
Design students, xviii
Design with Nature, 42
Detached single-family homes, 27, 28, 34, 35, 36, 70, 125
Detention basins, 61

Development costs
  amount to invest, 160–62
  builder size and, 161–62
  cash-flow analysis, 161, 162–63
  cheap houses vs. quality community, 155–56
  community investment benefits, 156–60
  fiscal impact analysis, 145
  mitigating, strategies, 35, 157–60
  premium charges contributing to, 157–58
  pro forma analysis, 91, 160–61, 171
  special district financing, 59, 163
  stakeholders, 146–49
Development suitability, 42. *See also* Environmental assessment
Direct service jobs, 22–23
Diversity, 15
  advantages, 5, 15, 39, 100, 124, 157
  in blended communities, 124
  cluster designs and, 33
  contrast/color and, 107
  example communities, 115, 125, 126
  footprint orientations and, 38
  as goal, 102
  lack of, 12
  lot/product types and, 28
  neighborhood compatibility and, 17, 100
  open space and, 117
  TND and, 119
  value and, 13, 28
Dry utilities, 61

E

Economic base analysis, 20, 21–23
Environmental assessment, 42–57
  climate, 51–52

Street design
 balancing factors, 5
 considerations, 59
 decreasing vehicle concentration, 59
 slope and, 47, 48–49
 traffic-calming devices, 59
 vehicular connections, 17, 117, 128
Street music, 106, 107
Stub streets, 33, 173
Subdividers, 14, 155
Suburban sprawl. *See* Sprawl
Summary vision document, 90–91

T

Tallyn's Reach (CO), 69, 94–96
Taxes
 balancing land use for, 145
 building industry contributions, 148
 fiscal impact analysis, 145
 increasing revenues from, 140, 141, 145
 for infrastructure, 59–61, 140, 148
 special district financing, 163
Tax Increment Financed (TIF) bond, 59–61, 163
10,000-square-foot Lots, 29–31
Texture, 105–6
Themes, common, 16
Three-story walkups, 37
TIF. *See* Tax Increment Financed (TIF) bond
Timeline, 11

TND. *See* Traditional neighborhood development (TND)
Topography, xix, 4, 9, 15, 27, 28, 118
Topo tables, 168
Townhomes, 27, 35
Traditional neighborhood development (TND), 34, 117–19, 122, 124, 125, 127
Traffic circles, 59
Transect, rural to urban, 108–9
Trees. *See* Vegetation
Tree wells, 68
Tuck-under garages, 31, 33

U

Urban cottages, 34
Urban infill. *See* Infill (urban) development
Utilities. *See* Infrastructure; Dry utilities

V

Vegetation, 4. *See also* Natural environment
 cooperative programs for, 149
 inventorying site, 53
 low-impact development, 68–69
 preserving, 52–54
 tree wells, 68
 wildlife and. *See* Wildlife
Vehicular connections, 17, 117, 128
Veterans Administration, 11
Views, 55–56

The Village at Autumn Lake (WI), 49, 50, 70, 83–88, 119–22, 123
Visioning. *See* Community visioning
Visual environment, 13, 106

W

Walkout units, 29, 31, 32, 33, 37, 48–49, 147
Water. *See also* Hydrology
 on-site systems, 61
 service analysis, 59–61
 sewer and, 59–61
Water-quality ponds, 5, 49, 120, 174
Welwyn Garden City (England), 7–9
Wetlands, 15
 as amenities, 49, 51
 boardwalks in, 109, 120
 constructed, 62
 example communities, 111, 115, 120
 maps of, 42
 mitigation banks, 51, 149
Wildlife, xix, 4
 Ahwahnee Principle, 134
 maintaining habitat, 15, 41, 54–55, 134
 water, wetlands and, 51, 68, 70, 109, 111
Windler Homestead community (CO), 64–65, 66, 67

Z

Zero lot line, 32, 174